PATHS

to

HAPPINESS

50 WAYS TO ADD JOY TO YOUR LIFE EVERY DAY

EDWARD HOFFMAN, PhD

CHRONICLE BOOKS
SAN FRANCISCO

For Daniel and Sophia

Text copyright © 2016 by Edward Hoffman.

Library of Congress Cataloging-in-Publication Data
available.

ISBN 978-1-4521-4907-3

Manufactured in China

MIX
Paper from
responsible sources
FSC
www.fsc.org
FSC™ C008047

Designed by Debbie Berne

10 9 8 7 6 5 4 3 2 1

Chronicle books and gifts are available at special
quantity discounts to corporations, professional
associations, literacy programs, and other organizations. For details and discount information,
please contact our premiums department at
corporatesales@chroniclebooks.com or
at 1-800-759-0190.

Chronicle Books LLC
680 Second Street
San Francisco, California 94107
www.chroniclebooks.com

ACKNOWLEDGMENTS

This book would not have been possible without the guidance of others. I wish to thank my editor, Lisa Tauber, for enthusiastically shaping and bringing this project to Chronicle Books, where her colleagues Rachel Hines and Dawn Yanagihara brought it smoothly to completion. Christina Ip has been an energetic research assistant. In offering extensive conceptual contributions and graciously critiquing my writing, Eric Freedman has been a valuable friend, as always. I have enjoyed stimulating conversations with Catalina Acosto-Orozco, Tony Bevacqua, William Compton, Marcos Florence, Jenniffer Gonzalez Mujica, Aaron Hostyk, Jenny Isaacs, Susan Kaneshiro, Neal Kaunfer, Fernando Ortiz, Paul Palnik, Shoji Muramoto, and Kirk Schneider related to diverse topics in this book. The opportunity to teach positive psychology at Yeshiva University for the past five years has immeasurably broadened my knowledge of this subject. My oldest son, Jeremy, has been a font of encouragement, and Daniel and Sophia have been my daily cheerleaders at home. Above all, I would like to thank my wife, Elaine, for her conceptual advice, patience, and unflagging support throughout this project.

CONTENTS

INTRODUCTION

∿

DO YOU KNOW what really makes you happy? If so, could you describe it clearly to a close family member or friend? Would you have used the same words five or ten years ago, or have life events significantly changed your viewpoint? More broadly, what do you think brings genuine happiness to most people? Are we all uniquely different in this regard, or pretty much the same the world over?

Everyone seems to have ideas about this topic, and it's been that way for millennia. The biblical Book of Psalms, attributed to King David, celebrates, "This is the day that the Lord has made; let us rejoice and be glad in it." A bit more pragmatically, the Book of Proverbs asserts, "A cheerful heart is good medicine, but a crushed spirit dries up the bones." As for the ancient Greek philosophers, virtually every major thinker from Aristotle and Socrates to Plato and

Sophocles weighed in on the subject too. Anyone who tells you that the desire to be happy has mainly been a twenty-first-century concern is badly mistaken.

However, there's now a lot more scientific knowledge about happiness than you might suspect—and more than has ever existed before. Although William James, the visionary founder of American psychology, argued more than a century ago that "there is no happiness without action," few of those who followed in his field actively researched the matter, until quite recently. They had minimal interest in studying joy, merriment, or contentment; instead, they mirrored Sigmund Freud's focus on darker aspects of human nature. Indeed, even when Freud wrote about humor, he saw it in essentially negative terms—as veiled hostility. As you'll see later in this book, scientific experts today know that laughter can be quite healthy, and even therapeutic.

While it's certainly not necessary to be a professional psychologist to hold valid opinions about happiness, I believe that my long career as a researcher and writer, therapist and educator has equipped me well to

present important findings in positive psychology—
and, equally vital—to give specific advice. In this book,
I offer fifty different avenues to enhance your daily
well-being. This list, of course, isn't intended to be
exhaustive. Certainly, there are other constructive
paths to happiness that I could also have highlighted—
but, alas, some of these have garnered meager scientific support to date.

I've deliberately chosen topics that involve happiness in a deeper sense—that is, happiness derived from
finding meaning and self-fulfillment. This approach
is based on my conviction that joy comes from expressing our creative and spiritual potentials to the fullest,
as well as from self-direction and warm relations
with others. For this reason, you'll find topics such as
awe and prayer, dreams and nostalgia, friendship and
mentoring. The fifty chapters, each covering a single
topic, are arranged in alphabetical order, beginning
with Acting Improv and ending with Zen Meditation,
and each concludes with a guided activity.

Studies suggest that you're likely to find this
book deeply satisfying. There's ample evidence that

satisfying self-reflection and journaling elevate our mood, bringing greater life contentment. You may also use this book as an opportunity to affirm your most significant values and interests. Additionally, if you have children, nieces or nephews, or grandchildren, this book will provide an especially meaningful way to share happy memories and new experiences with them.

Depending on your current interests, you may find yourself drawn to particular topics and eager to explore their personal relevance. Other topics may appeal to you less. That's perfectly fine. I don't expect that all fifty themes will speak to your soul. But having personally discovered new paths to well-being, such as birding and gardening, by researching this book, I can attest that it is advantageous to have an open-minded, adventurous attitude.

Now have fun!

1

ACTING
IMPROV

· · ● · ·

"ONE OF THE things I learned from improvising is that all of life is an improvisation—whether you like it or not," observed Alan Arkin. The Oscar-winning actor found his true calling through improv—performing on stage without a script—over fifty-five years ago. A cofounder of Chicago's famous Second City comedy troupe, Arkin strongly advocates improv in actor training—and enhancing personal growth for all. In his book *An Improvised Life*, he recounts how improv activity taught him vital lessons about emotional honesty, spontaneity, and effective listening—and making him a happier person.

Though Arkin's praise for improv is based mainly on personal experience, health professionals are increasingly adopting his view. Scientific evidence remains scarce, yet the experience of interacting spontaneously with others before an audience seems to increase self-confidence, social ease, ease of decision making, creative thinking, and teamwork ability. In this light, Dr. Allen Cornelius at Denver's University of the Rockies offers workshops called "Improv Your Counseling," in which counselors perform improvisatory exercises to strengthen their skills in listening, attending to nonverbal cues, and mirroring (reflecting back what they're hearing and seeing). Cornelius discovered a link between improv and therapy while researching the psychological benefits of humor. Therapy and improv are similar, says Cornelius, "[because it's] two or more people cooperating in a process that's uncertain, likely has unexpected twists and turns that each party must adapt to, and works toward a satisfying conclusion." In Chicago, the Panic/Anxiety/Recovery Center recently partnered with Second City to offer an eight-week program using improv to help adults overcome their social anxiety.

Managerial professionals are also joining the bandwagon. Kip Kelly at the University of North Carolina's Kenan-Flagler Business School promotes improv as a tool for leadership training, "as its activities and exercises are easy to implement, and they provide tools, tricks, and techniques that individuals can practice and refine." Major companies such as GE, McDonald's, Nike, and Pepsi have introduced improv into management training, for example, to heighten sensitivity to diversity. Improv has even helped physicists at the European Organization for Nuclear Research, known as CERN, hone their communication and listening skills.

It's not surprising that improv activity produces emotional and social benefits: It's an informal cousin to the professional practice known as *psychodrama*. Developed in the 1920s by Dr. Jacob Moreno, the method uses role playing—often in groups—to spur emotional growth. Guided by a trained therapist, the group enacts dialogues or scenes related to a member's fears, fantasies, or life events. Suppose, for example, that Sara is a young woman stressed by her domineering parents. The therapist might ask Sara to reenact their last argument, with two group members assigned to play her parents. As the scene unfolds, she would be encouraged to identify all her thoughts and feelings—thereby gaining insight into the troubling relationship. She would also be guided in replaying the scene several times to strengthen her self-confidence in relation to her parents.

continued ➡

Improve with Improv

· · · · · · · · · · · · ·

Join an improv class or workshop. Experienced actors say you'll gain the most if you follow these five tips:

1) At the outset, establish the setting: Where and when is the action taking place? Keep this reality constant.

2) Understand your character's motivation; why are you doing what you're doing?

3) Connect with the other players by focusing on your relationship with them.

4) Listen and react to what's actually said rather than to what you're expecting.

5) Don't try to be funny. Let the scene unfold spontaneously, and always strive to tell the audience a story. It's all about storytelling.

2

ADVENTURE
SPORTS

· · ● · ·

"SPORT HAS ENORMOUS power to sweep us beyond our ordinary sense of self, to evoke [hidden] capacities," reported Michael Murphy, cofounder of California's famous Esalen Institute for personal growth. His groundbreaking 1995 book *In the Zone*, written with Rhea White, drew upon thousands of accounts, from both professional and weekend athletes, revealing the power of sports to enhance our well-being. In the ensuing twenty years, several research areas have emerged related to Murphy's interest—ranging from the study of "peak performance" (as it's known in sports psychology) to nature-based adventure.

Peak performance involves top achievement, whether in a solitary sport such as diving or a team effort like football. In interviews with hundreds of athletes for their book *Peak Performance*, Dr. Charles Garfield and Hal Bennett found that eight conditions accompany those moments when athletic activity is optimal:

1. mental relaxation and a sense of calm

2. physical relaxation with loose, fluid movements

3. self-confidence and optimism

4. a focus on the present moment

5. a high energy level, along with feeling "charged up"

6. extraordinary awareness of one's body

7. a sense of total control without undue effort

8. being "in the cocoon," that is, in a mental envelope protecting the athlete from distractions

Sounds wonderful, doesn't it? Not surprisingly, peak performance has aroused interest from everyone wanting to "get into the zone" athletically—or just gain a competitive edge. Browse the Web, and you'll find sites offering peak-performance training for basketball, golf, soccer, lacrosse, volleyball, motocross racing—and nonsports such as real estate sales. In the late 1990s, research led by Dr. Susan Jackson of Australia's University of Queensland showed that flow is a key aspect of peak performance. Ever since, training has focused on maximizing that inner state. How? Particularly through meditation, exerting mental control over distractions, and effective preparation for competitions.

Since Murphy's influential book appeared, nature-based or "adventure" sports have gained the attention of health researchers. Reflecting his yoga study in India, Murphy was fascinated by the transcendental accounts of deep-sea divers, hang gliders, and mountain climbers, "where silence is part of the environment." What motivates such practitioners? As reported in *Sport and Exercise*, Drs. John Kerr and Susan Mackenzie found a wide range of motives, often intertwined—including goal setting, risk taking, escaping boredom, socializing with friends, pushing personal boundaries, and overcoming fear, as well as bodily delight from moving in water or air, and bonding intensely with nature. As a middle-aged champion kayak racer explained to the researchers, "For me, there was that whole combination of a beautiful river, challenging grade, and just feeling that [my] body was moving quite elegantly and fluidly."

Among today's leaders in scientifically studying such activities is Dr. Barbara Humberstone of Buckinghamshire New University in England. In her view, adventure sports such as scuba diving, long-distance cycling, and windsurfing are important sources of well-being because they bond us with nature in "kinetic empathy." The key isn't that the activity be high risk, but that it attunes our mind and body with the natural world.

Get Adventurous Outdoors

Adventure sports often require physical stamina, so be sure you're medically cleared beforehand. Whatever the activity, here are five tips:

1) Choose an outdoor setting that fits your personality. Some people adore flowing water, others snowy surroundings.

2) Check the weather and dress appropriately. Even in the summer, the mountains can be cold.

3) Start slowly and let yourself build endurance.

4) Venture outside your "comfort zone" only when you feel ready.

5) Keep things social. You'll get more out of your experience when sharing it with others.

ART APPRECIATION

· • ● • ·

FOR CENTURIES, ART galleries and museums have delighted people throughout the world—including Sigmund Freud, an impassioned museum-goer drawn especially to antiquities on his Italian trips. Nevertheless, Freud never analyzed art appreciation as a source of well-being. Nor did protégés such as Otto Rank, who wrote insightfully about the creative process in his book *Art and Artist*. As you'd expect, opinions in the literary world have been more plentiful. Edgar Allan Poe opined that great art evokes tears by revealing our distance from the divine, while Tolstoy extolled art as empathy building. For Virginia Woolf, artistry sharpens our sensitivity to beauty in everyday life.

Are such views true? Until recently, almost no scientific theory or research existed, but the situation is changing. Dr. James Pawelski at the University of Pennsylvania's Positive Psychology Center is studying how people experience art in museums. "When you go to the library," he explained to a *New York Times* reporter, "you don't walk along the shelves looking at the spines of the books and on your way out tweet to your friends, `I read 100 books today!' You can't really see a painting as you're walking by it."

For Pawelski, the solution is simple: Slow down. He recommends that gallery-goers spend at least twenty minutes in front of a single painting they find intriguing—and in this way, really experience it.

In a study, Daniel Fujiwara at the London School of Economics analyzed the reports of over 14,000 British adults on their involvement in culture and sports. After controlling for many factors, he found that museum visiting enhanced both happiness and self-reported health. Surprisingly, his overall sample valued this activity more than playing a sport, doing artwork, or attending sports events or concerts. Interestingly, those who as children never visited museums with their parents were unlikely as adults to do so.

How does museum-going benefit mind and body? An answer may lie in Attention Restoration Theory, first formulated by Drs. Rachel Kaplan and Stephen Kaplan at the University of Michigan during the 1980s. They were initially interested in how natural settings help people overcome mental fatigue and related feelings of irritability and stress. In their view, hiking or strolling through nature elicits four payoffs: (1) *fascination*, or engaging our attention in an effortless way; (2) *being away*, or removing us from daily routines and demands; (3) *extent*, or experiencing a venue with enough structure and scope to occupy our mind for hours or longer; and (4) *compatibility*, or being in a place that's a good fit with our interests and goals.

As researchers like Dr. Jan Packer of Australia's University of Queensland have argued, art museums often offer these same restorative qualities, thereby enhancing well-being and satisfaction. Especially for people who live in urban settings, that's an important consideration.

Take a Good, Long Look

. . . .

On your next visit to an art museum or gallery, spend at least twenty minutes with each of two works of art you find intriguing. Then immediately write about what resonated with you—and what feelings were evoked. Why do you think these works moved you strongly?

AUTHENTICITY

· · ● · ·

"TO THINE OWN self be true," declared Shakespeare's Polonius to his son Laertes in *Hamlet*, "And it must follow, as the night the day, Thou canst not then be false to any man." Penned in the early 1600s, the Bard's famous words have inspired parental advice for centuries, yet still remain relevant for daily living. In our own time, it was Dr. Carl Rogers who first advanced the concept known as *authenticity*. As a cofounder of humanistic psychology, he stressed the importance of precisely this trait—recognizing and expressing one's true feelings. This principle came directly from Rogers's pioneering work in what he termed "nondirective counseling" during the post–World War II era. When his clients succeeded

in dropping their social masks, they felt happier and
more energized.

Later, Dr. Clark Moustakas of Detroit's Merrill-
Palmer Institute applied the notion of authenticity
to education and related fields. In his view, authentic
teachers help students to develop their interests instead
of merely memorize facts. He also linked authenticity
to creative achievement, and he decried the imperson-
ality of our educational system, in which both teachers
and students are viewed as basically interchangeable,
rather than as unique individuals. More recently, Dr.
C. Terry Warner of Brigham Young University has highlighted the dangers of self-deception and self-betrayal
as spillovers from inauthenticity. That is, when we act
in ways contrary to our true self, our ability to lead a
satisfying, productive life is undermined; we become
our own worst enemy. Drawing upon philosophy and
religion, Warner argues that the surest path to joy is
always to be straightforward with others.

Several contemporary researchers have created
detailed models of authenticity. Dr. Alex Wood at
the University of Stirling in England utilized three

dimensions taken directly from Rogers's theory: self-alienation, authentic living, and conforming to external influences. For Wood and his colleagues, authenticity means that we're aware of our inner reality, able to express ourselves in accordance with our true self, and resistant to pressures of conformity. Dr. Michael Kernis and his then-graduate student Brian Goldman at the University of Georgia at Athens mapped authenticity on four other dimensions: *awareness* of one's feelings and motives; *unbiased processing*, or seeing oneself without biases or illusions; *behavior*, or acting in ways consistent with one's values and beliefs; and *relational orientation*, or striving to be open and genuine in one's relationships.

The ancient Delphic temple in Greece was inscribed with the maxim "Know Thyself." But is authenticity really so important—or is this just a platitude? Recent research definitely links the trait to such features of well-being as life satisfaction, secure self-esteem, autonomy, and even mindfulness. All this makes sense, of course—for, as Moustakas advised, "When we're not honest, we're cut off from a significant resource of ourselves, a vital dimension that's necessary for unity and wholeness."

Hamlet's Polonius would surely have agreed.

Get to Know Yourself

· · · · · · · · · · · · · ·

Since authenticity is always rooted in self-knowledge, these questions are helpful:

* As a child, what did you want to be when you grew up, and what did that goal mean to you? Is it still relevant in some way?

* What makes you laugh? The ancient Jewish Talmud says that what we find funny is highly self-revealing.

* What activities do you enjoy, and are these mainly solitary, duo, or group?

* With whom can you "be yourself" most easily? Who do you feel really accepts you without judging or categorizing you?

5

· · ● · ·

"AWE IS A way to wisdom," declared Abraham Joshua Heschel. "Awe is more than an emotion. It is a way of understanding, an act of insight into a meaning greater than ourselves." One of the twentieth century's leading theologians, Rabbi Heschel regarded awe as vital to self-fulfillment and the basis for a satisfying life. Until recently, psychologists have devoted little attention to this trait. Yet, as far back as the early 1900s, William James viewed our capacity to experience awe—such as in contemplating the vast mysteriousness of the universe—as fundamental to the "healthy-minded soul."

With the advent of positive psychology, researchers have become increasingly interested in experiences of awe. Dr. Dacher Keltner of the University of California at Berkeley found that these are often catalyzed by encounters with nature or art, as well as observations of human excellence such as Einstein's discoveries or Mozart's musical compositions. Paradoxically, it seems, such experiences leave us feeling small before a greater vastness, yet more connected with all around us. San Francisco's existential theorist Dr. Kirk Schneider has written extensively about the role of awe in optimal psychological functioning—and its link to empowering feelings of adventure and discovery.

The emotion of awe has probably never been commonplace, but perhaps it's particularly elusive in today's fast-paced society. Thanks to the Internet, there are now countless distractions to garner our attention, if only fleetingly—until the next stimuli arrive as photos, video clips, texts, or email. Sure, they may be momentarily entertaining. Yet, not only do these offer a paltry sense of transcendence, they actively inhibit its possibility.

So what's the antidote? How can we achieve greater awe in daily life?

In Schneider's view, it's vital to cultivate these six conditions:

1. *Time for reflection.* That is, simply having a potent or even extraordinary experience isn't sufficient. We must be able to ponder or "process" it, and this can't be done overnight.

2. *The capacity to slow down.* It's a stark commentary on our era, but this essentially passive capability for many of us needs to be learned as an almost Zen-like practice.

3. *The capacity to savor the moment.* Indeed, the concept of savoring has become important in positive psychology. That is, full experiencing with sensory delight.

4. *A focus on what one loves.* It may seem surprising, but such a focus remains rare. The more we concentrate on what gives us joy, the greater our likelihood of awe.

5. *A capacity to see the big picture.* Yes, everyday living is filled with mundane details. But if all we do is micromanage ourselves and others, how can we encounter awe?

6. *An ability to trust in the ultimately knowable.*
Perhaps more than these other conditions, this
one involves risk taking and a leap of faith. Why?
Because experiences of awe don't require logical
explanation, only our openness to larger meaning.

Opening to Awe

Because the individual triggers for this exalted
emotion vary from one person to another, it's
important to identify the experiences in which
you've personally felt this sense of marvel.
When did you most recently feel awe, and what
induced it? Were you alone or with other people? In light of Heschel's view, what experiences
have given you a sense of life's mysteries—of
what he called "wide horizons [and] intimations
of the divine"? Coupled with the six conditions
described above, such self-knowledge will help
you to build awe more powerfully into your
daily life.

BiRDING

· · ● · ·

"ONE NOTE FROM one bird is better than a million words," mused Emily Dickinson in one of her many unpublished literary pieces. Among America's most revered poets, Dickinson lived in Amherst, Massachusetts, all her life, and rarely left her father's small farm. Over a thirty-six-year period ending with her death in 1886, she wrote nearly 1,800 poems, few of which saw print until years later. Quite a careful bird-watcher, she knew intimately their songs, habits, and traits—and her poems reflect this interest. It's estimated that more than 250 of them mention birds, with twenty-four different species named. Some are rare around New England today—bluebirds, bobolinks, cuckoos, meadowlarks, and whip-poor-wills—due to big land developments that replaced fields and orchards. But other species, including cardinals and mockingbirds, are now more common, possibly due to climate change.

Dickinson's fascination with birds transcended books, for no ornithological pocket guides existed during her lifetime. In 1834, the naturalist-explorer Thomas Nuttall authored the first such work, illustrated with woodcuts. Among its most original features was his careful attempt to describe birdsongs through syllabic patterns. But it was hardly a concise field guide, composing a massive two-volume set.

In 1889, the first popular book on birding was published in the United States. Written by naturalist Florence Merriam Bailey, *Birds Through an Opera Glass* was a portable guide and, with the use of binoculars, made it possible to identify birds in the field without first shooting them. Written in a chatty style to entice readers to venture outdoors, *Birds Through an Opera Glass* described seventy species and helped launch popular interest in bird-watching as a healthful and conservation-minded activity. As part of this trend,

President Theodore Roosevelt in 1908 compiled a list of ninety-three species of birds he'd seen in the environs of Washington, D.C.

According to a recent survey conducted by the U.S. Fish and Wildlife Service, 46 million Americans engage in bird-watching; of these, only about one person in eight can identify more than twenty species. The vast majority are home birders, people who maintain bird feeders and enjoy identifying species in their own yards. This was undoubtedly the case for Dickinson, whose lifetime preceded the establishment of the National Audubon Society and the growth of birding groups.

Though poets for millennia have extolled birds for their beauty and song, surprisingly little scientific study has been undertaken regarding their effect on our well-being. Among today's leading investigators is Eleanor Ratcliffe at the University of Surrey in England. In recent research funded by Britain's National Trust and the Surrey Wildlife Trust, her team found that birdsongs and birdcalls helped people to reduce both stress and cognitive fatigue. However, as you might suspect, not all such sounds were perceived as soothing. Those produced by some species—such as crows, magpies, and owls—were regarded unfavorably, with negative appraisals like "raucous" and "squawking." Overall, the researchers concluded that certain sounds were restorative depending on their particular acoustic properties, especially tuneful songs with minimal repetitiveness.

Birding Basics

Birding requires minimal basic equipment. You'll need a notepad, a field guide for your area, and a reliable pair of binoculars. Dress comfortably and appropriately for the season. Many bird-watchers like to take photographs, which helps with species identification, especially if the bird quickly flies away. When setting up, be quiet and prepared to remain a while. Such patience allows birds to become accustomed to your presence and helps overcome their skittishness.

7

COMMUNITY SINGING

· · ● ··

"WITHOUT MUSIC, LIFE would be a mistake," wrote Friedrich Nietzsche. Though the great German philosopher was cynical about many things, music was not among them. As a youth, he learned to play piano and ardently composed music set to his poems, such as *Hymn to Friendship.* Later, he became close with the composer Richard Wagner—and, as a renowned professor at the University of Basel, enjoyed playing four-handed piano with his best friend, the theologian Franz Overbeck. In Nietzsche's view, music not only exalts us emotionally, but it also sharpens our intellect. "Has one noticed," he asked in an 1888 letter, "that music frees the mind, lends wings to thoughts, so that one becomes a philosopher all the more? [When I hear

Bizet's music], answers fall into my lap, a minor hail-
storm of ice and wisdom, of solved problems."

Several founders of psychology avidly performed
music publicly. Alfred Adler delighted in singing folk
tunes of his native Austria, as well as Franz Schubert's
romantic *lieder* for voice and piano. As a teenager,
Abraham Maslow studied the piano and was an
impassioned Carnegie Hall attendee. In the early 1930s,
he planned his master's thesis on the psychology of
music, but his professors vetoed the topic as unscientific. Indeed, nearly forty years would elapse before
the American Association for Music Therapy was
established, and then additional decades followed,
until significant research on music and positive
psychology—especially related to group singing—
took place around the world.

Betty Bailey and Jane Davidson at the University
of Sheffield in England reported the results of interviews with Canadian choir singers from both impov-
erished and middle-class backgrounds. The researchers
discovered that group singing produced the same
beneficial mental and emotional payoff regardless of

participants' social class or musical training—even when "the sound produced by the vocal instrument was of mediocre quality." In the context of mediocre singers, how about karaoke? From extensive fieldwork in Japan, Dr. Hideo Watanabe of William Patterson University in New Jersey found that participation in karaoke clubs had a variety of cognitive, emotional, and social benefits—especially for older Japanese persons.

Among today's leaders in this musical field are Stephen Clift and Grenville Hancox at Christ Church University in Canterbury, England. For over a decade, they've been investigating the effect of group singing on personal well-being. As reported in *Music Performance Research*, their study of over 1,100 choral singers in Australia, England, and Germany revealed that community singing produced benefits including:

- greater happiness and better mood
- improved attention and reduced rumination (improved attention and reduced fixation on past emotional hurts)

- deeper breathing, which heightened fitness and lessened anxiety

- enhanced social support, as choral singing is an intrinsically cooperative endeavor; many friend-ships emerged from it

- cognitive stimulation and a sense of achievement

- motivation to stay physically active because choral singing requires regular practice and a commitment to attend rehearsals

This last issue, of course, becomes increasingly important for well-being during the later years.

continued ➡

Join a Choir

. . . .

What type of choir most interests you?
Options include large-scale classical concert
groups and choral societies, often with an
orchestra; religious choirs, which may perform
traditional sacred music or gospel; or community groups, frequently sponsored by continuing
education programs. Not all choirs require
auditioning—so if the thought makes you nervous, don't worry; you'll likely find a suitable
setting without doing so. For many choirs, you
needn't know how to read music. Their members learn the notes together as a group. Find
a group with a schedule that's doable for you—
and start harmonizing!

8

COOKING
AND BAKING

· · ● · ·

"THE MEASURE OF achievement is not winning awards. It's doing something that you appreciate, something that you believe is worthwhile," Julia Child advised. "I think of my strawberry soufflé. I did that at least twenty-eight times before I finally conquered it." The popular TV chef and author who adapted complex French cooking for everyday Americans first discovered the joy of cooking as a bored housewife in post–World War II Paris. Married to a U.S. diplomat, Child initially tried hat-making and bridge to ignite her enthusiasm before discovering her life-dream at a Cordon Bleu cooking class. Well into midlife, she coauthored *Mastering the Art of French Cooking* in 1961, debuted a cooking class on Boston TV the following year, and became a familiar figure for decades on shows like *Good Morning America*.

Despite Child's popularity, American psychologists had long viewed cooking and baking as basically mundane chores for women—and hence, hardly worthy of serious study. A conceptual breakthrough occurred when the Czech Dr. Mihaly Csikszentmihalyi (originator of the influential concept of *flow*, or pleasurable absorption), examined the daily logs of more than ten thousand people over a twenty-year period. In 1990, he reported in his book *Flow* that of the sixteen most common daily activities that produced flow experiences, cooking ranked seventh—behind only lovemaking, socializing, talking, eating, engaging in sports, and shopping, in that order. The prevalence of transcendence in kitchen activity didn't surprise Csikszentmihalyi, who after that study boasted to a *New York Times* journalist, "I can lose myself in making a Bolognese sauce, finely chopping the onions, the carrots, three kinds of meat, and the slow, slow simmering. There's a sense of order and control, and something so wholesome and tactile about cooking."

With the rise of the Food Network and celebrity chefs, popular periodicals including the *Wall Street Journal* and *Forbes* have increasingly touted the mental health benefits of kitchen activity—and linked it to today's wider positive psychology movement. Dr. Todd Essig, a psychoanalyst and professor at New York Medical College, has developed the concept of "culinary mindfulness." Rather than relying on America's powerful fast-food industry for dictating our attitudes toward meals, Essig insists, it's imperative for our health that we develop a new viewpoint. Instead of mindlessly grabbing processed foods such as chips to consume while watching television, we need to savor each phase—from meal purchasing and preparation to the final act of eating.

Empirical studies in the kitchen are sparse, but Lesley Haley and Elizabeth McKay in Britain interviewed hospitalized mental health patients in occupational therapy baking groups. As reported in the *British Journal of Occupational Therapy*, four main benefits emerged:

1. "Not playing Scrabble again," involving a sense of purpose in meal production

2. "Chocolate chip biscuits don't come only in boxes," relating to a sense of accomplishment

3. "Christmas past, present, and future," encouraging critical thinking about the occupational therapy program

4. "Too many cooks," focusing on feelings of belongingness and camaraderie generated by group baking. Overall, baking proved a strong motivator and confidence builder.

Kitchen Adventures

Cooking needn't be complicated or expensive. First, get the right utensils and optimize your kitchen. Keep it tidy and, whenever possible, clean as you cook to avoid a post-meal letdown. There are countless blogs and cookbooks out there. You might want to start with a favorite family recipe and invite someone to dine with you. Foodies advise that for beginners, breakfasts are easiest—scrambled eggs, anyone?

9

CREATIVITY

· • ● •·

"CREATIVITY IS JUST connecting things," Steve Jobs told *Wired* in 1996, at a time when he was seeking to regain leadership of Apple, the company he cofounded. "When you ask creative people how they did something, they feel a little guilty because they didn't really do it—they just saw something. . . . They were able to connect experiences they've had and synthesize new things." Jobs may have been deliberately elusive or modest in his explanation. But as the driving force for Apple's transformation into the world's richest, most-admired company, he's now viewed as the exemplar of creativity—and executives everywhere are seeking people with his remarkable mindset for innovation.

Not surprisingly, an entire mini-industry of coaches and trainers has arisen promising to teach managers, engineers, and others how to be more creative. At the same time, major corporations like Google are increasingly using creativity tests in employment interviews—hoping to discover the next Steve Jobs before their competitors do. Hiring fads come and go regularly in business, but what do psychologists really know about creativity?

More than fifty years ago, Dr. Joy Paul Guilford argued that creativity is based on "divergent thinking" and comprises four distinct abilities: (1) *fluency*, quickly producing many ideas or solutions; (2) *flexibility*, simultaneously proposing a variety of approaches to a specific problem; (3) *originality*, producing new ideas; and (4) *elaboration*, systematizing an idea to make it a reality.

While at the University of Southern California, Guilford developed tests to measure divergent thinking—what's popularly known as "thinking outside the box"—and his approach still dominates the field. More recently, Dr. Dean Simonton of the

University of California at Davis offered a useful distinction between *big C* creativity (that influences the world, like the invention of the telephone) and *little c* creativity (involving everyday problem-solving, like finding a better route through the morning's commute, or adapting well to a job change). In Simonton's view, these two types of creativity may comprise differences of degree along the same continuum.

Can creativity be taught? The scientific evidence seems to answer *yes*. In a review of over 150 training programs, Dr. Ginamarie Scott Ligon at the University of Oklahoma and her colleagues found that well-designed programs produce real gains—and the skills generalize across settings. Interestingly, her team found that programs teaching divergent thinking and problem-solving strategies are more effective than those involving self-expression or imagery practice. Such research confirms Guilford's view that creativity depends more on learning to think differently than on simply "letting it all hang out."

Aside from improving work success, creative thinking seems to be linked to happiness. It may also be an effective antidote to boredom—a psychologically unhealthy state linked to health problems ranging from substance abuse to depression and obesity. In this light, a research team led by Dr. Timothy Wilson at the University of Virginia found that people prefer performing mundane activities—and many even prefer self-administering electric shocks—to sitting alone in a room with nothing to do for fifteen minutes. We can't all be Steve Jobs, but probably everyone can learn to think more creatively and keep boredom at bay.

Common Objects, Uncommon Ideas

. . . .

To enhance divergent thinking, choose a common object and identify as many different uses for it as possible. Because your goal is learning to "think outside the box," let yourself describe highly unusual uses. Give yourself fifteen minutes for this task, and select a different object each day of the week.

Generate uses for:

1) a flowerpot
2) an umbrella
3) a book
4) a pencil
5) a rubber band
6) a hat
7) a paper clip

10

CURIOSITY

$\cdot\cdot\bullet\cdot\cdot$

DO YOU HAVE many interests, or only a few? Do you enjoy exploring new places? At work, do you get bored quickly when everything's familiar? Such questions center on curiosity—a personality trait gaining increasing attention in positive psychology and its spinoffs in business, education, entertainment, and science. As Dr. Carol Greider of Johns Hopkins University, winner of the 2009 Nobel Prize in Physiology or Medicine, observed about her own work on chromosomes, "New discoveries come from the most unlikely places. Curiosity-driven research provides unexpected discoveries that have implications for human health."

Historically, of course, many inventors and scientists—ranging from Marie Curie to Thomas Edison—have insisted on the importance of curiosity as a force for innovation. One of the most popular film-makers of our time, Steven Spielberg, told an audience of graduating college students, "The greatest quality that we can possess is curiosity, a genuine interest in the world around us. The most used word—and I have five kids, so I know what I'm talking about—is *Why?* From this simple question and such basic curiosity, great acts are born."

Only since the early 2000s have psychologists probed curiosity as a specific trait—partly because it's hard to separate from other traits, such as focusing ability. Dr. Todd Kashdan of George Mason University has been a leading researcher in this specialty. He helped develop the first scientific scale to measure curiosity—and then applied it experimentally. With colleagues, he found that high scorers showed greater playfulness, wit, and ability to bond emotionally with a stranger of the opposite sex than did low scorers. Highly curious people also gave more attention to their assigned partners during their conversation. In brief, curiosity seemed to be an asset during the fledgling stage of romance. More recently, Kashdan's research team also found that highly curious people were less emotionally aggressive toward their romantic partner than their less curious counterparts. Why? Presumably because they weren't as self-centered and defensive.

Curiosity also seems beneficial cognitively. As reported in *Neuron*, Dr. Charan Ranganath of the University of California at Davis and his colleagues asked participants to review more than one hundred trivia questions, such as, "What does the term *dinosaur* actually mean?" and "What Beatles single lasted longest on the charts?" Participants rated each question as to how curious they were about the answer. Then, while the researchers scanned their brain activity using an MRI machine, participants revisited each question and waited briefly for the answer, while a photo of a face totally unrelated to the task flashed before them. Afterward, the researchers tested to see how well participants recalled and retained both the trivia answers and the faces they saw. Ranganath's team found that greater interest in a question—that is, curiosity—predicted better memory not only for the answer, but also for the unrelated face that had preceded it. A day later, the results still held. Somehow, curiosity prepared the brain for learning and long-term memory more broadly.

Banishing Boredom

Select a country that you've never visited, but which you're curious about. Over the next three weeks, learn about its history; culture, including traditional and current music and arts; cuisine; industry; politics; and natural environment. Keep a notebook to jot down intriguing topics from your Web explorations, and a folder for downloads. You'll gain new knowledge and generate further interests. When ready, decide if you'd like to plan a visit—and what you'd most like to see or do there.

11

DANCING

• • ● • •

CAN DANCING BE a metaphor—and a prescription—for personal well-being? In the popular Japanese movie from the '90s *Shall We Dance?* (later remade by Hollywood), that is the message. Shohei Sugiyama is a successful Tokyo accountant with a wife and daughter, but he has become joyless. His life is on a downward emotional spiral, and his family is concerned. By taking ballroom dancing lessons at a studio—secretly, because such behavior is unconventional for a Japanese man of his social stature—Sugiyama regains his happiness and strengthens his family too. Despite its arcane subject of ballroom dancing in Japan, *Shall We Dance?* struck a chord for many viewers around the world.

Of course, dancing has been prized for millennia by diverse cultures and spiritual traditions for its exalting effects. From the whirling dervishes in Turkey and Central Asia to Native American shamanism, dance has been regarded as an inspirational, even sacred, human activity. Perhaps because none of psychology's founders were interested in dancing (although Alfred Adler treated the distressed, celebrated ballet performer Vaslav Nijinsky, to meager result), the first major professional organization devoted to this field—the American Dance Therapy Association—wasn't established until 1966.

The association's stated mission is to promote "the emotional, cognitive, physical, and social integration of the individual." Its practitioners use dance/movement therapy (DMT) to treat depression and dementia among adults, as well as, more recently, autism-spectrum disorders and learning disabilities in children and teens. Dr. Christina Devereaux of Antioch University, a specialist in this field, has noted, "The major strength that dance/movement therapy has in working with people with autism is its ability to produce [positive] outcomes in the area of social relatedness—especially in the formation of relationships."

It's not surprising that dancing can be therapeutic for persons with health-related ailments, but can it also enhance general well-being? As reported in *Arts & Health*, Dr. Cynthia Murcia of Germany's Goethe University and her colleagues analyzed the reports of 475 nonprofessional dancers. Most practiced more than one genre (folk dance was most popular, followed by ballroom and disco) and averaged eighteen hours monthly. Overall, they reported emotional, physical, social, and even spiritual benefits—as well as higher self-esteem and better ability to cope with daily stress. Those who spent more time in dance practice reaped greater benefits than their less-involved peers. As in research findings on group singing, women recounted a greater payoff from dancing than did men.

Are some dance styles more rewarding than others? Scientific evidence isn't yet definitive, but Murcia and associates in another study found that twenty-two tango dancers had lower levels of stress hormones after dancing with partners, and also felt more relaxed. Meanwhile, at Australia's University of New England, Dr. Rosa Pinniger's team reported in *Complementary Therapies in Medicine* that men and women who participated in a six-week tango class increased their mindfulness more than control-group or standard mindfulness-training peers.

Invitation to Dance

You'll find classes at dance schools and studios, as well as health clubs, recreation centers, YMCAs, and some religious institutions. First decide on a dance style, whether ballet, folk, or belly dancing. Visit a few venues while they're in session and see how you like the ambience. After you find a promising one, meet the instructor and check out costs, which can vary widely. Once enrolled, wear suitable clothing for your classes and try a few dancing styles until you find your niche.

DOING ART

· · ● · ·

FEW IN RECORDED history have shown Michelangelo's remarkable talent in painting and structure. Yet even he wrote, "The true work of art is but a shadow of the divine perfection." Philosophers through the ages have valued art as a medium of self-expression. Indeed, from the inception of modern psychology in the nineteenth century, its leading thinkers have not only been fascinated by art but actively engaged in it themselves for the joy it evoked.

The young William James ardently studied painting in both New England and Europe before finally choosing medical training instead, at Harvard in 1861. His youthful drawings, which still exist, reveal a talent for both portraiture and still life—the latter prominent in James's journals while traveling through Brazil with naturalist Louis Agassiz some years later.

After breaking bitterly with Freud in 1913, psychiatrist Carl Jung, then in his late thirties, painted in his private journal to help regain emotional stability. Recently published as *The Red Book* (*Liber Novus* in Jung's Latin nomenclature), his journal reveals vivid mythological images in intense, bold colors. For Jung, art was a vital path for healing and growth.

Another major theorist attracted to art was Erik Erikson, who helped originate the study of personality development throughout life. After graduating from high school in Germany, he roamed through Europe in the mid-1920s—bartering or selling his sketches for sustenance—before enrolling in a German art school. In his capacity as a children's art teacher, he gained the attention of Anna Freud, who eventually brought him into her father's influential circle. Though Erikson wrote little explicitly about art, he extolled children's creative playfulness as a desirable trait at all ages— and regarded artwork as a valuable therapeutic tool.

Rollo May, a founder of existential psychology, was also initially motivated to become a professional artist. Though he shifted his career focus, May retained a lifelong interest in the creative process. His final book, *My Quest for Beauty*, revealed how aesthetics had always been a "redemptive" force for self-fulfillment. "Artists . . . love to immerse themselves in chaos in order to put it into form, just as God created form out of chaos in Genesis," May wrote in his book *The Courage to Create*. "Forever unsatisfied with the mundane, the apathetic, the conventional, they always push on to newer worlds."

It hardly seems coincidental that psychologist Mihaly Csikszentmihalyi, who originated the concept of *flow*, as a young man was passionately drawn to art, and came to regard aesthetic activity as a model for healthy absorption. In this light, the American Art Therapy Association (AATA)—the major professional organization in the field for decades—is moving beyond its traditional focus on treating disability and mental illness to a broader emphasis on using art to enhance well-being. In a 2013 article published in

AATA's journal, Rebecca Wilkinson and Gioia Chilton proposed the launching of a new specialty, which they called "positive art therapy." What are its goals? To foster happiness, flow, and positive emotions—such as hope, joy, and even love—through art making.

Get Wet with Watercolors

Watercolor painting is relaxing—and also intriguing due to the pigments' accidental effects and unpredictable behavior. To start, just add water to paint and put brush to paper. Remember, the paint will always look more intense when wet, so test your colors on a separate paper before using them. Be sure to use a good brush that'll retain its shape with fine brush marks. As watercolor papers vary widely in both thickness and texture, you'll enjoy experimentation.

13

· · ● · ·

DO YOU FIND dreams intriguing? Has a dream ever inspired, excited, or worried you? If so, you're hardly alone, for nearly every culture in recorded history has valued dreams as a source of well-being. During their golden age, the ancient Greeks built more than three hundred temples in homage to their god of healing, Asclepius. Supplicants would travel long distances and participate in sacred rituals designed to elicit a useful dream. In the Orient, dream-incubation temples were erected in serene and peaceful settings. On our own continent, Native American tribes valued dreams as a wellspring of sacred guidance. Their shamans would journey deep into the wilderness, and, depriving themselves of food, water, and companionship, they'd induce a dream of power or knowledge to take back to their people.

The Jewish spiritual tradition, dating back to the Bible, is filled with references to the visionary power of dreams, such as those of Joseph and Daniel. In later centuries, Kabbalists valued dreaming for self-knowledge and linked particular images to their symbolic importance. As rabbi-physician Solomon Almoli explained in his influential *Pitron Ḥalomot* (*Interpretation of Dreams*) published in 1515 in Greece, "Know that a dream can bring awareness only after it has been interpreted; otherwise, the dream is meaningless."

With the rise of the Industrial Age, such intuitive wisdom fell on hard times. When Sigmund Freud began to research the medical literature of his day for information on dreams, he found that almost nothing had been written on the topic. Most of his colleagues viewed the whole matter as superstition, unworthy of serious attention. Indeed, when he published his landmark *The Interpretation of Dreams* in 1899, he was greeted with professional ridicule and derision. For several years, his cogent probings on the connection between dreams and personality were dismissed as the ravings of a madman or a pornographer.

Eventually, the psychoanalytic movement that Freud spearheaded gained momentum and helped restore in Western culture a strong interest in dreams. Though nearly all of Freud's early associates—such as Alfred Adler, Carl Jung, and Theodore Reik—diverged from their mentor's emphasis on sexuality in creating their own psychological systems, they shared his admiration for dreams as "the royal road to the unconscious." For example, Adler analyzed dreams for messages regarding issues of power, Jung probed for spiritual awakenings, and Reik sought signs of grappling with creative expression.

More recently, the existential psychologist Rollo May argued that dreams reflect how we both experience and give meaning to our world. In his view, our dream life reveals our outlook and deepest concerns. Though every dream has its own theme, May contended, dreams often run together in series—reflecting an overall view of life. For existential psychologists today, like Drs. Ed Mendelowitz and Kirk Schneider—both faculty at Saybrook University in San Francisco—the goal of dream interpretation isn't triumphantly to explain "what it means" but to expand the dreamer's self-awareness, so that what's occurring within can be felt more deeply or with greater clarity.

Explore Your Dreamworld

To keep a dream journal, get a separate notebook and place it beside your bed at night. As soon as you awaken, write down your dream, as it may fade after only a few minutes. Mark the date and recount your dream using the present tense ("I am running in a race") to increase its vividness. Note how you felt when you awoke from it. You needn't share *every* dream, but it's useful to have a partner to enhance your motivation and help your interpretation.

EMPATHY

· • ● • ·

DO YOU EASILY know what others are feeling? Do people say that you're a "good listener"? Do you also have the ability sometimes to experience their varying moods as your own? If so, then you are strongly empathic—and this gift has probably served you well throughout life. Why? Positive psychology is increasingly viewing empathy as a trait vital for both happy and successful living. Not only does research reveal that empathy is a unique glue for binding friendships, family ties, and romantic love, it even improves our work achievement. Certainly this makes sense, for without adequate empathy, we're unlikely to know what animates our coworkers, clients, or customers.

These recent findings are a big change from the earlier idea popularized by Dr. Richard Dawkins of Oxford University, that everyone is born with a dominant "selfish gene." Many evolutionary scientists now argue, instead, that positive inborn emotions like altruism and empathy—and not greed and selfishness—have enabled our species to survive and prosper. Such a view also repudiates the Freudian emphasis on human darkness.

No baby can possibly live without caring, nurturing adults there on a daily basis. As the Austrian physician Alfred Adler asserted more than seventy-five years ago, children's empathy must be nurtured or it remains weak. Though there is clear evidence that girls are more empathic than boys by early childhood, both genders can enhance this trait through positive books and films. Research led by Dr. Jessica Stern at Pomona College showed that parents who are empathic toward their children ("I see you're feeling sad. What happened today at school?") are more likely to strengthen empathy in their offspring.

Can a person have too much empathy? From my experience as a psychologist, the answer is *yes*. Without even knowing it, some people are "emotional sponges"—constantly absorbing the feelings of others who are sad or distressed, and then keeping those feelings bottled within. Highly empathic people, who often choose work in the helping professions, must learn to become resilient. How? Two good ways involve setting clear boundaries between themselves and clients, and making time for emotional "seclusion" to self-recharge.

But most of us have the opposite problem: We're not empathic enough, and there's a real price we pay for that weakness. Our friendships, family relations, and romantic love all suffer when we lack sufficient empathy. Recent studies have clearly linked romantic satisfaction to good empathy between both partners. Our spiritual life also benefits from an empathic attitude toward others. The ancient Talmud declares, "When two people listen patiently to each other, God listens to them too."

Albert Einstein expressed a similarly mystical view of the universe. Comparing the isolated self to a prison, he declared that, "Our task must be to free ourselves by widening our circle of compassion to embrace all living creatures and the whole of nature in its beauty." Perhaps it was psychologist Carl Rogers who said it best: "When a person realizes he has been deeply heard, his eyes moisten, as if weeping for joy. It is as though he were saying, `Thank God, somebody heard me. Someone knows what it is like to be me.'"

Cultivate Closeness

Looking back on your life, think of an episode when a friend's empathic word or glance uplifted your mood. Next, recall an episode when the empathy you expressed toward another made a big difference. Finally, select a day to become more consciously empathic in every conversation—and notice the results.

15

EXPLANATORY STYLE

· · ● · ·

"LOOK FOR THE Silver Lining," urged the popular song by Jerome Kern and George DeSylva in 1919. As successful, New York–born sons of foreign immigrants, both shared a buoyant optimism about life and expressed it through music. The world's most horrendous war had just ended, leaving more than thirty million casualties, but the song's upbeat tune and lyrics advised to "always find the sunny side of life" and look for golden rays behind clouds. Though this approach is often criticized as a naïve, uniquely American viewpoint, it's strongly supported by positive psychology. Research clearly shows that our *explanatory style* (how we interpret bad events that happen to us) has important consequences for our mental and even physical health.

A leading figure in emphasizing the value of an optimistic explanatory style has been Dr. Martin Seligman of the University of Pennsylvania. During the mid-1980s, he studied the explanatory style of major league baseball players and managers. By analyzing their public utterances reported in hometown newspapers, he found that "optimistic teams" did better than their previous win-loss records would objectively suggest and that "pessimistic teams" did worse.

In the same period, a study of the National Basketball Association reported similar findings: For both individuals and teams, an explanatory style existed that could be identified and measured. And, crucial in Seligman's view, these styles predicted victory, above and beyond sheer athletic ability. How so? Because playing-field success was related to optimism, whereas failure was related to pessimism.

Subsequently, Seligman and his colleagues found that a pessimistic explanatory style was a major risk factor for physical illness. In a fascinating study involving physical and mental health data from Harvard classmates during World War II, Seligman's research team was able to retrospectively determine that explanatory style affected students' later health from ages thirty to sixty. Those who were pessimistic as young adults were significantly more likely to have poor health during this age bracket than those with a sunny outlook.

According to Seligman, our explanatory style comprises three distinct aspects. These relate to:

1. *Permanence.* Does one believe that the distressing situation will always exist or that it will be only temporary? One person experiencing a job loss or divorce may feel sure that the stress will never end, whereas her friend may see the identical situation as short-lived.

2. *Pervasiveness.* Does one view the unpleasant situation as all-encompassing or as specific in nature? One college student who fails a required course may give up on everything, whereas another might simply appraise whether to shift to another major.

3. *Personalization.* Does one blame oneself entirely for a bad event, or spread the blame to others? As you might suspect, it's not psychologically healthy

to engage in self-berating whenever something goes wrong. As the sculptor Auguste Rodin observed in teaching his talented student Malvina Hoffman, "Nothing is a waste of time if you use the experience wisely."

Learning from Your Past

· · · · · · · · · · · · · ·

Recall a past experience that turned out badly for you—perhaps a vacation, a college course or job, a friendship, or a romantic fling—and for which you've often blamed yourself. After recounting the debacle, consciously change your habitual self-talk. First, affirm that the event happened and is over; it is no longer occurring. Second, recognize that it was confined to only a small part of your life. Finally, determine that the result wasn't 100 percent your fault by identifying a person or circumstance that was also responsible—and let it go. You're likely to feel happier!

Eχpressive Writing

· • ● •·

"I NEVER TRAVEL without my diary," quipped the writer Oscar Wilde. "One should always have something sensational to read in the train." Though few of us have lives as rich in stunning dramatic events as Wilde's was, his regard for journaling would be embraced by today's positive psychologists. Regardless of one's literary talent, the practice known as *expressive writing* has increasingly proven a valuable tool for personal well-being.

Among the founders of this approach was Dr. Ira Progoff, a New York psychotherapist who did his doctoral thesis on Jungian psychology. Completed in 1951, the thesis so impressed the eminent Carl Jung that he invited Progoff to study with him in Switzerland.

Their years together greatly influenced Progoff—and later, at New Jersey's Drew University, he conducted research on how people develop more fulfilling lives. Strikingly, he found that those involved in journaling resolved their emotional problems more rapidly than nonjournalers. Building on this insight, Progoff in the mid-1960s developed a system that he called the Intensive Journal Method. Popularized through workshops and books, it initially comprised a binder-and-loose-leaf-paper format of sixteen sections for writing about one's life, including turning points and dreams, and also utilizing inner dialogues.

For more than twenty-five years, Dr. James Pennebaker at the University of Texas at Austin has led scientific study on the benefits of expressive writing. His first book, *Opening Up: The Healing Power of Expressing Emotions*, highlighted its usefulness for people suffering from trauma, especially with unexpressed feelings of shame or humiliation that had been kept secret. He later extended his findings to such painful life experiences as divorce and job loss. As Pennebaker explained in an interview, "Emotional upheavals touch every part of our lives. You don't just lose a job; you don't just get divorced. These things affect all aspects of who we are—our financial situation, our relationships with others, our views of ourselves. . . . Writing helps us focus and organize the experience."

In Pennebaker's view, the act of writing about a painful experience is generally more effective for self-healing than talking about it. Why? Writing necessarily requires that we put our thoughts into a coherent pattern—and thereby helps us to emotionally distance and "process" the event so that it loses its enslaving power. As Sigmund Freud discovered to his initial surprise, replaying a traumatic event in our mind doesn't end its impact. Unless it's accompanied by insight, catharsis isn't really a path to cure.

How about expressive writing concerning happy events? In an interesting study led by Dr. Sonja Lyubomirsky of the University of California at Riverside, people who systematically analyzed their most joyful days showed *lower* well-being and physical health—they felt worse, not better! In contrast, those who simply recounted enjoyable memories without dissecting them reaped benefits. The overall research evidence therefore seems clear: Analytically writing about a traumatic or upsetting experience helps us to dissipate it, but doing so with an exhilarating memory is counterproductive—so just bask in its glow.

Write Away

Each day for a week, write about something from your past that made a big impression on you emotionally. It's especially helpful to recount an event that still resonates for you in some way. Whether you're describing a joyful or a sad experience, don't worry about style or literary quality. As novelist and impassioned diarist Virginia Woolf declared, "The habit of writing thus for my own eye is good practice. It loosens the ligaments."

· · ● · ·

"IT'S AS IF everything is happening in slow motion,"
says National Basketball Association superstar Kobe
Bryant, "and you just really want to stay in the moment.
You don't want to step outside of yourself, because then
you're going to lose that rhythm." In quite a different
vocation, the artist Paul Klee described the process:
"Everything vanishes around me, and works are born
as if out of the void. . . . My hand becomes the obedient
instrument of a remote will."

Though you may be neither a professional athlete
nor an artist, you may at times have been so absorbed
in an activity that you "lost yourself" happily—and
time seemed to disappear. If so, you're no stranger
to the experience of *flow*, the focus of much research

today for its personal as well as organizational benefits. Because such moments in the workplace are linked to greater engagement and productivity, business leaders are especially interested in this intriguing phenomenon. Their goal? To help spur and sustain flow experiences in everyday activities.

Though it might surprise you, this psychological concept is unrelated to the once-popular maxim "Go with the flow." Rather, it was developed by Dr. Mihaly Csikszentmihalyi after years of study based partly on his own life experience. Born in 1934 in Hungary, he spent part of his childhood in a prison camp during World War II, where he discovered that chess enabled him to transcend the horrendous suffering around him. As Csikszentmihalyi later recalled in an interview, "It was a miraculous way of entering into a different world where all those [terrible] things didn't matter. For hours, I'd just focus within a reality that had clear rules and goals." When he took up painting as a teenager, he found that this activity, too, evoked a delightful sense of absorption, and after gaining his doctorate at the University of Chicago in 1965, he conducted pioneering studies of artists and other highly creative persons. Eventually such research led to the concept of flow—which he defined "as a state in which we're so involved in an activity that nothing else seems to matter; the experience is so enjoyable that people will continue to do it even at great cost, for the sheer sake of doing it."

How do you know when you're in a flow experience? Csikszentmihalyi has identified eight features:

1. a merging of action and awareness, so that you're fully "inside" the activity
2. complete concentration on the task at hand, thereby transcending all distractions
3. no worry about losing control
4. a loss of self-consciousness, in which your ego is quieted or united with something greater
5. an experience that time passes unusually, generally described as either "speeding up" or "slowing down" tremendously
6. The experience is autotelic—that is, done for its own sake—rather than as a means to an end.

7. The experience involves a skillful activity, particularly in which you're challenged slightly beyond your normal skill level.

8. The activity has clear goals and provides immediate feedback. You know what you're supposed to accomplish and you're not left guessing about your performance. Competitive sports fit this last feature quite well.

Get into the Zone

. . . .

To increase flow in everyday living, choose activities that are fun, mildly challenging, and involve a sense of mastery. If the activities are too easy, you'll get bored quickly. Too hard, and you'll become frustrated and quit. Clear goals are also important. Avoid times when you're feeling tired or rushed. Finally, minimize distractions in order to concentrate fully, and you're on your way.

18

FORGIVENESS

· • ● •·

IS IT EASY for you to forgive others, or rather difficult? Do you often have thoughts of gratitude about your life at present, or do you fixate on past experiences when people have disappointed you? Finally, are you able to forgive yourself for old mistakes? Today, such questions are a major focus of positive psychology. Scientific evidence increasingly shows that forgiveness is vital for our emotional and our physical well-being.

It's hardly coincidental that the world's great spiritual teachers for millennia have extolled this value. Both Eastern and Western traditions honor the ability to let go of feelings of anger and hurt about the past, and venerate the sage as one who is free of such shackling emotions. Drawing on millennia of religious teaching, Dr. Martin Luther King asserted, "We must develop and maintain the capacity to forgive. He who is devoid of the power to forgive is devoid of the power to love." Likewise, Mahatma Gandhi declared, "The weak can never forgive. Forgiveness is the attribute of the strong."

Learning to forgive isn't always easy. Many people seemingly get stuck between wanting to do it and actually being able to. Dr. Robert Enright of the University of Wisconsin at Madison, a leading researcher in this field, proposed that forgiveness involves four steps:

1. *uncovering* one's emotions of anger or resentment
2. *deciding* to forgive
3. *working* to reframe an incident through insight and empathy
4. *deepening* one's sense of meaning as a result of one's injury

By following through on these steps, people can lower their worry and distress.

Scientific evidence is mounting about the health benefits of forgiveness. People who have forgiven others for a major transgression have lower blood pressure and heart rates as compared to those who remain unforgiving. Dr. Kathleen Lawler-Row of East Carolina University in Greenville, North Carolina, extensively studied the impact of both hostility and forgiveness on the human body. In one investigation, she found that sleep quality—which has been found to affect many aspects of health—is influenced by the tendency to have thoughts of revenge. As you might guess, people with bitter thoughts were more likely to suffer from insomnia than those whose minds were at peace. Similarly, a team of New York University researchers found that cardiac patients with forgiving personalities had less depression and anxiety about their condition, lower blood pressure, and better cholesterol levels than their less-forgiving peers.

Psychological research, intriguingly, shows that women are more likely than men to forgive others, due to greater empathy—but women are less likely to forgive themselves. As we get older, we generally tend to become more forgiving. Why? Apparently because with increasing chronological age, we see the "big picture" of life in better perspective—a quality vital for wisdom. In this sense, the ability to forgive is a strength we should all develop to gain new opportunities for happiness. As the American diarist Paul Boese aptly remarked, "Forgiveness does not change the past, but it does enlarge the future."

Let a Resentment Go

What kinds of acts do you find it easiest to forgive in yourself and others? What things are more challenging for you, and why? In your view, are certain acts unforgivable? And finally, can you identify a resentment within you, and let it go today?

19

FRIENDSHIP

• • ● • •

HOW ARE YOU when it comes to friendship? Is there someone with whom you share your life's joys and disappointments? Can you always count on this person to be loyally by your side, or only in fair weather? Is your relationship one of unconditional trust, or do you each often withhold facts and feelings from the other? Such questions are intriguing for most of us to ponder. Further, according to mounting evidence from psychology and medicine, their answer holds a key to our wellness, vitality, and longevity.

Though behavioral scientists for the past generation have affirmed a measurable link between friendship and well-being, the concept is hardly new. Indeed, the Greek philosopher Aristotle addressed the topic nearly 2,500 years ago in his major work on ethical conduct and character virtues, *Nicomachean Ethics.* In a highly influential formulation, he distinguished among three types of friendship—based on *utility,* on *pleasure,* or on *virtue.* Those composing *utility* were basically business relations, with mutual tangible benefits such as money or power. Friendships based on *pleasure* were founded on fun interests, such as attending sporting events or concerts together. For Aristotle, *virtuous* friendship was the highest of the three—involving emotional concern and compassionate care. In his view, friendship based on *virtue* had the greatest impact on human well-being in everyday life.

Aristotle's outlook was extended during the Middle Ages by the influential rabbinic scholar-physician Moses Maimonides. Living in Spain and Egypt more than eight centuries ago, he asserted that friendship is vital for individual wellness. In a treatise of health advice written for a young prince in Saladin's royal court, Maimonides advised: "It is well known that one requires friends all his lifetime. When one is in good health and prosperous, he enjoys the company of his friends. In time of trouble, he is in need of them. In old age, when his body is weak, he is assisted by them."

Since the advent of behavioral medicine in the mid-1970s, investigators have closely studied what is known as *social support*. From the inception of this exciting field, they've differentiated *instrumental* support from *emotional* support—that is, caregiving help involving tangibles such as money or food, cooking or housecleaning, from such intangibles as empathy and advice.

Increasingly, researchers have come to focus on one specific aspect—the confidant relationship— because of its importance for our well-being. The range of studies has been wide, from drug abuse and depression among American and Canadian teenagers to health practices among young Mexican men. Repeatedly, research shows that having a trusted friend with whom to share emotions lessens virtually all forms of risky and self-destructive behavior. Studies also demonstrate that people with a confidant have better physical health—and are less likely to suffer from a variety of chronic medical problems. Such individuals also show greater emotional resilience and less vulnerability to depression. As reported by Dr. Paul Surtees and his colleagues at Strangeways Research Laboratory in England, there's evidence that having a confidant can add four to five years to one's life. Not a bad payoff at all.

Celebrate a Confidant

Whom do you most trust in sharing your intimate feelings, your joys, frustrations, and decision-making plans? When and how did you first become friends, and what keeps you emotionally close? To help strengthen your bond, be selective about what you unburden, as venting about your smallest emotional hurts is unproductive. Be sure to express gratitude to your friend, for no one wants to feel exploited by others.

20

GARDENING

· · • ··

"THE GARDEN IS quite a love," Jane Austen gushed in a letter to her older sister, Cassandra. "I go and refresh myself now and then, and then come back to solitary coolness." The celebrated writer not only filled such novels as *Pride and Prejudice* with gardens as a literary device but cherished them in her own tumultuous life. The Austen family moved several times—tending gardens in both town and country. After her father's death in 1805, Jane relished extended visits to her brother Henry's London home with its lavish garden surrounded by fields.

Many English writers, like Jane Austen and D. H. Lawrence, featured gardens as colorful backdrops for everyday life, special social events—and of course, romance. But it was the American physician Benjamin Rush, a signer of the Declaration of Independence, who first documented the health benefits of gardening. As surgeon and psychiatric director of Pennsylvania Hospital, he reported that working with plants and soil helped patients stay calm and constructively engaged.

For more than a century, gardening was regarded professionally as beneficial mainly as an adjunct treatment for mental illness. However, the rehabilitative care of hospitalized World War II veterans expanded acceptance of what came to be termed *horticulture therapy* (HT). By the 1980s, HT practice had gained considerable credibility and was embraced by a variety of therapeutic disciplines. Psychological research showed that HT improves concentration and memory, language skills, and motivation. In vocational training, it helps people to follow directions, solve problems, and work independently. And in physical rehabilitation, HT has proven effective in strengthening patients' muscles and improving balance, coordination, and endurance.

Though it hasn't remained my specialty, I co-authored with David Castro-Blanco a seminal study of horticulture therapy with a preschool child. Months of traditional play therapy involving doll figures had gone nowhere with Josh (not his real name). But he responded remarkably well to guided caring for a small plant in our therapy room. Over a few weeks, Josh saw with delight how his efforts enabled the plant to grow and thrive—and one day, he happily announced: "Just like I'm helping the plant, you're helping me to act bigger!" After this insightful remark, Josh's progress accelerated—and in his final session, he took his beloved plant home. In this light, it seems no coincidence that the idea for positive psychology came to its founder, Dr. Martin Seligman, in an "aha" moment while gardening with his then-young daughter.

An especially interesting new trend is "therapeutic gardens." Advanced by landscape architects for health-care settings, the purpose is to enhance the well-being of patients, residents, and clients, as well as visitors and staff. According to horticulture therapist Teresia Hazen, "[These] provide safe, secure, and comfortable [settings]. . . . The provision of shade and other protective structures, the flourishing plants, and the protected and protective nature of the therapeutic garden offer personal comfort and refuge to the garden user."

Jane Austen would heartily agree—and perhaps add a suggestion about potential romance as well.

Bonding with Herbs

For indoor herb gardening, all you need is a sunny, warm place and containers large enough for your plants to grow. Prepare your containers by filling them with good soil and fertilizer according to package directions. Mix in water until the soil feels damp all the way through. Whether planting seeds or transferring your plants from their starter containers, be sure to provide ample sunlight daily and not to overwater. Later, you'll need larger pots because the herbs will eventually outgrow their originals.

21

GENEALOGY

· • ● •·

"HISTORY REMEMBERS ONLY the celebrated; genealogy remembers them all," quipped indie movie actor and writer Laurence Overmire. Born in upstate New York, he began in the 1990s to research his family history—a project that not only uncovered several *Mayflower* passengers in his ancestry and created databases to aid other heritage seekers but also led to the first, joyful Overmire family reunion in over one hundred years. Such results are typical in this realm—and as revealed by the popularity of TV shows like *Finding Your Roots* and *Who Do You Think You Are?*, millions of people today are seeking precisely such connections in our fragmented society. Such programs typically feature a world-famous individual who finds new life meaning through ancestral investigation.

Of course, you needn't be a celebrity or have a celebrity ancestor to reap benefits from genealogical activity. Rather, there's increasing scientific evidence that tracing one's family history has a significant psychological payoff. Among the first researchers to show this was Pamela Drake, who, in 2001 at the State University of California at Fullerton, surveyed more than 4,100 people involved in genealogy. She found that their generativity (concern for future generations) improved as they became more involved in genealogy, with activities such as preserving family memorabilia and conducting oral histories. In addition, they strengthened their "sense of place"—that is, personal connectedness to a particular locale or social community. Contrary to popular stereotype, most were not isolated oldsters seeking to pass time, but middle-aged married people—typically beginning their genealogical activity at age forty.

More recently, Dr. Robyn Fivush at Emory University and her colleagues have verified the importance of family history for adolescent identity and well-being. In a series of studies involving both preteens and teenagers, they found that participants who scored higher on the twenty-item "Do You Know" scale of family history were psychologically healthier and more resilient than their less heritage-aware peers. Specifically, the more family-knowledgeable youngsters had a stronger sense of self-identity, higher self-esteem, less anxiety, and a lower likelihood of both "acting out" and negative, internalizing behaviors such as depression. Not surprising to the researchers, those with higher scores on the "Do You Know" scale reported better relations among family members—and more frequent sharing of family history.

This test asks children and teens such yes/no questions as: Do you know how your parents met? Do you know where your parents were married? and Do you know which person in the family you look most like?

Apparently, even thinking about one's forebearers has psychological benefits. As reported by Dr. Peter Fischer at Austria's University of Graz and his colleagues, college students who spent five minutes thinking about either their fifteenth-century ancestors or their great-grandparents were more confident about their exam-taking ability than those asked to recall a recent shopping trip. Positive differences also emerged concerning verbal and spatial intelligence tasks. Describing such results as evidence for what they called "the ancestor effect," the researchers speculated that thinking about our family history strengthens our sense of personal identity—and thereby enhances self-confidence.

Uncover Your Roots

Genealogy is all about family connection, so a useful starting point is to interview an older relative—ideally, face to face. Get a notebook or audio recorder and be sure to mark the date. Begin with factual questions, such as birthplace and year, education, occupation, and other bio data. Then elicit information about ancestors, including reminiscences. If you find yourself "warming to the chase," ask for permission to make copies of relevant documents and photos, and get names of additional relatives to contact.

22

GRATITUDE

· · ● · ·

WHAT ARE YOU most thankful for in your life? How often do you feel grateful, and how easy is it for you to express gratitude? It's not surprising that such questions have become vital to the new field of positive psychology, for gratitude has been a valued emotion throughout human history in diverse cultures. Gratitude is cherished in Buddhist, Christian, Jewish, and Muslim religious tradition—and nurtured by prayer and service to others. A Talmudic legend recounts that, by divine punishment, King Solomon was cast down from his throne and forced to wander for several years as a beggar until he appreciated what he *had*, instead of complaining about what he *lacked*. The ancient Roman philosopher Cicero declared, "Gratitude is not only the greatest of virtues, but the parent of all the others."

Yet, until recently, psychology had remarkably little to say about this trait. An exception was the theorist Abraham Maslow, who became convinced—based on his studies of self-actualizing men and women—that the abilities to both feel and express gratitude easily are vital aspects of mental health. Similarly, he viewed ingratitude as a disturbance. During the 1960s, Maslow taught methods for nurturing gratitude, such as recalling the joys of one's life and also imagining that one has only a short time left on earth. In Maslow's view, the ancient adage "Count your blessings" remains highly relevant.

During the past fifteen years, psychological research has emphasized the importance of gratitude. It's now clear that grateful people are generally happier people. They also have greater optimism and life satisfaction. But which causes which? In an interesting experimental study, Dr. Jo-Ann Tsang at Baylor University found that people who received a favor helped more and reported more gratitude than those who randomly received a positive outcome. Such studies suggest that gratefulness is a quality formed through our social relations—and not in isolation. In other words, those with a strong sense of gratitude have probably been treated kindly while growing up, and are therefore more likely to act thankfully.

We also know that people who feel thankful toward their romantic partner or friends report greater satisfaction. They feel closer and experience less conflict. Certainly, these scientific findings make sense, for if you've a strong, positive emotion like gratitude toward a key person in your life, you're less likely to harbor anger or disappointment. Increasingly, marriage and family therapists advise the practice of expressing daily gratitude to one's loved ones to strengthen bonds: Simple words can have profound effects.

Dr. Martin Seligman at the University of Pennsylvania and his colleagues have developed several methods for increasing well-being through gratitude. Among the most powerful is the "gratitude visit," in which one selects a living person to whom one is grateful—such as a former teacher, friend, or older relative—then writes a letter expressing this emotion, and hand delivers it to that individual. The "gratitude visit" has generated reports of beautiful and intense experiences, and boosted well-being even months afterward.

Take Time to Be Thankful

Each day for three weeks, put aside time to identify all the things for which you're grateful—such as your family and friends, health, home, possessions, talents, and interests. Each day, also recount something that occurred for which you're thankful. It needn't be big or dramatic. Then try the "gratitude visit," and see what happens.

23

HUMOR AND LAUGHTER

· · • · ·

HAVE YOU HAD a good laugh lately? Anything funny happen to you this week? What types of jokes make you chuckle the most? Such questions are increasingly the focus of scientific research—for evidence is now amassing that our sense of humor directly affects our well-being.

Despite the Hollywood stereotype of grim-faced shrinks, psychologists have been interested in this topic for over a century. A landmark was Sigmund Freud's classic 1905 book *Wit and Its Relation to the Unconscious*. In Freud's influential view, people use humor as an indirect way to express feelings that would otherwise be blocked by their unconscious mind. A good example is sarcasm, which Freud correctly saw as masked hostility. In his view, jokes allow our suppressed emotions to surface and be released—thereby ridding us of inner tension.

A longtime Freudian associate was Alfred Adler, who emphasized the importance of humor for well-being—and warned that it's never good to take oneself too seriously. "I can't deny that I tease my patients," Adler once confided at a training seminar, "but I do so in a friendly way. I like to show through a joke what's happening in a case. It's very worthwhile that you have a great collection of jokes. Sometimes a joke can help the patient see how ridiculous is his neurosis."

Later, psychologist Abraham Maslow wrote extensively about humor among highly successful people—those whom he termed *self-actualizing*. He noted that such persons richly enjoy humor, but of specific kinds: They share an appreciation for life's absurdities and the ability to laugh at their own foibles. They also shun jokes that are insulting, malicious, or cruel—that is, laughing at someone else's expense. The ancient Talmud advises that one of the best ways to discern someone's true nature is uncovering his or her sense of humor.

Today, positive psychology is giving much attention to humor, since having a healthy capacity for laughter seems an important aspect of well-being. In particular, Dr. Rod Martin at the University of Western Ontario and his colleagues have studied *humor styles* and garnered clear evidence that people differ in the role humor plays in their daily lives. Martin's work identifies four different types of humor:

1. *Affiliative*—which involves humor as an effective "social lubricant," such as in improving parties or other group gatherings

2. *Self-enhancing*—which relies on humor to cope effectively with stress, and is a form of resilience

3. *Aggressive*—which involves sarcasm and other hostile verbalizations to maintain a sense of superiority or entitlement

4. *Self-defeating*—which centers around self-put-downs and is the bulwark of countless comedians, from early Woody Allen movies to the latest *Saturday Night Live* incarnation

As you might suspect, the first two types of humor have been linked to good mental health. However, the latter two are associated with emotional problems, including chronic anger, low self-esteem, and depression.

See the Light Side

Can you change your typical humor style to one that's healthier, more fulfilling? Research is yet scanty on this question, but it would be wise to eliminate both aggressive and self-defeating jokes from daily conversations. It's also worthwhile to cultivate self-mirth—finding comical aspects in challenging or stressful situations. For example, think how a funny cartoon might depict it—and what might be the caption?

24

KINDNESS

· · ● · ·

"WHETHER ONE BELIEVES in a religion or not, and whether one believes in rebirth or not," declared the Dalai Lama, "there isn't anyone who doesn't appreciate kindness and compassion." Indeed, for millions around the world who probably know nothing about Tibetan Buddhism, this emphasis on altruism as a way of life has tremendous resonance. Although philosophers and spiritual teachers for millennia have articulated a similar message, social scientists have been late to the topic. The French sociologists Auguste Comte and Émile Durkheim introduced the concept of *altruism* (as an antonym of *egoism*) back in the nineteenth century, but psychologists essentially ignored it until twenty-five years ago.

Since then, the study of kindness has mainly followed two streams. The first involved "hero research"—focusing, for example, on the brave people who saved European Jews during the Holocaust, and on famous, exceptional altruists like Mahatma Gandhi and Mother Teresa. Though highly popular, such studies were largely anecdotal, with little scientific grounding. Only one consistent finding was rooted in objective measurement—that people with an "altruistic personality" scored higher in empathy than others.

The second research stream has used experimental situations—usually conducted with unsuspecting participants either on city streets or in psychology labs—to uncover why people behave altruistically and how it affects them emotionally. In this light, Dr. Sonja Lyubomirsky of the University of California at Riverside and her colleagues have found that performing acts of kindness boosts temporary happiness, as well as long-lasting optimism and well-being. Generally, too, adults who report that helping others is personally important as a guiding value are happier than those concerned instead with amassing wealth—or who are cynical about the existence of altruism. Such findings have been extended to childhood by Dr. Kristin Layous at the University of California at Riverside. In a large-scale study conducted in Canadian Vancouver with nine- to eleven-year-olds, those who performed three acts of kindness per week for a month raised their mood, life satisfaction, and peer popularity significantly more than did a control group.

Does simply witnessing kindness increase our altruism? As Cornell University researchers Drs. Milena Tsvetkova and Michael Macy reported in the journal *PLOS ONE*, the answer is no. When participants in their study observed a high level of helping, they were less likely to help another. Due to the well-known "bystander effect"—as it's called in social psychology—they felt their self-sacrifice wasn't needed. However, receiving help increased their likelihood of generosity toward a stranger—and weakened the tendency to disengage.

Since acts of kindness are easy enough, why aren't they more common? Research led by the late

Dr. Susan Nolen-Hoeksema of Yale University shows that *rumination*—thinking repetitively about past emotional hurts—is a chief obstacle. Not only does rumination carry risks for depression throughout life, but it's also linked to pessimism, self-criticism, and passivity. Such findings make sense, for it's difficult to act altruistically toward others when fixated on our own grievances. To reduce rumination and thereby maximize acts of kindness, psychologists recommend developing one or two favorite hobbies as distractions and writing expressively about the past painful event.

Surprise with a Good Deed

There are countless ways to act with unexpected kindness. Choose a day and perform altruistic deeds for three individuals—such as sending a gift book, baking or cooking a treat, or serving as a chauffeur. In doing so, make clear that no reciprocity is expected or desired.

25

KNIttING

· • ● •·

DO YOU ENJOY engaging in craftwork? How about knitting in particular? Traditionally linked to "women's skills" of home and hearth, craftwork is rapidly gaining the attention of wellness professionals. Recent research shows that, far from merely a quiet hobby, knitting produces a variety of health-related benefits—including stress reduction, mood elevation, pain management, and better motor coordination. As perhaps no surprise to your mother or grandmother, the bilateral, cross-midline, rhythmically repetitive, and autonomic nature of the movements are important, helping to induce feelings of deep calmness. It's no accident that the last few years have witnessed the publication of books such as *Mindful Knitting, Zen and* *the Art of Knitting*, and *Crochet Saved My Life*. In *Things I Learned from Knitting*, Stephanie Pearl-McPhee calls it "an excellent metaphor for much of life. Whether we like it or not, becoming knitters changes the way we think, feel, process information, and interact with the world around us."

Perhaps the most influential figure in today's "knitting and wellness" movement is England's Betsan Corkhill. A former senior physiotherapist, she left her country's National Health Service in 2002, frustrated by its bureaucratic structure that hindered effective treatment. Quitting her profession after much soul searching, Corkhill became a freelance production editor for a range of crafts magazines. Among her tasks was to read the large number of letters daily arriving at the office. She later reminisced: "About 98 percent of these talked about the therapeutic benefits of craft, but in particular knitting. That was my 'lightbulb' moment. I realized that I'd stumbled across something potentially very important . . . [both for] long-term medical conditions [and] as a springboard to other activities." In 2005, she founded Stitchlinks, a global support group for those who enjoy the therapeutic benefits of crafts, especially knitting.

Besides creating the Stitchlinks website and launching a variety of research projects, in 2012 Corkhill established the world's first conference on therapeutic knitting. Its aim? To spur both professional and public awareness about the health benefits of knitting. Since then, researchers have been actively examining the advantages of knitting for personal well-being.

Dr. Yonas Geda of the Mayo Clinic and his colleagues found that knitting was among the activities that helped reduce the likelihood of mild dementia among seniors—perhaps because crafting serves to build up cognitive reserves and the ability to buffer and withstand the presence of toxic chemicals in the brain. *The British Journal of Occupational Therapy* recently presented findings in which over 3,500 knitters responded to a survey developed by Jill Riley at Cardiff University in Wales. More than 80 percent reported themselves as feeling happier after knitting. Within the therapeutic realm, psychologists like Dr. Susan Kaneshiro of California are increasingly utilizing knitting as a therapeutic adjunct. In her view, knitting "helps promote mindfulness and effectively reduces anxiety. I also encourage people to join knitting groups, as these improve socializing in a pleasant, easygoing way."

Rhythms of Craftwork

If you haven't yet learned knitting or crocheting, it's useful to find a teacher. Many yarn stores offer public classes or sponsor events in which people engage in craftwork together. These provide good opportunities to acquire a mentor, for they draw persons at varying levels of ability. Be aware that in the final stage of a knitting project, you'll be obliged to shift from rhythmic, autonomic movements to those more complex, such as movements involved with sewing. It may be less satisfying momentarily, but you'll have something permanent to share.

26

LEARNING A FOREIGN LANGUAGE

· · ● ··

"EVERY LANGUAGE IS a world," declared the French-American literary critic George Steiner. "Without languages, we would inhabit parishes bordering on silence." Raised in the 1930s by a Bohemian father and Viennese mother apt to, in Steiner's words, "begin a sentence in one language and end it another," he was reading Shakespeare in English and Homer in ancient Greek by the age of five. With such training, it's not surprising that, as a professor at the University of Geneva in Switzerland, Steiner lectured in four languages—and as author of *Babel* produced a tour-de-force history of translation. Its central theme? That "each human language maps the world differently"—and provides a boundless potential for revealing dreams, geographies, myths, and reality itself.

Though few of can boast a Steiner-like polyglot upbringing, his advocacy for multi-tongued proficiency is gaining increasing support today. A growing number of universities throughout the United States now sponsor foreign language programs for adults in midlife and beyond, and popular magazines such as *Time* and *Forbes* regularly feature articles with titles like "Why Learning a Language Could Save Your Career." Reasonably enough, they argue that in today's increasingly global economy, people with competency in only one language are at a definite competitive disadvantage. The investment firm Goldman Sachs has reported that over 50 percent of its employees speak a second language, and that fluency in either Mandarin Chinese or German is especially advantageous. Now that Latinos compose more than 16 percent of the U.S. population, according to the 2010 U.S. Census, Spanish proficiency is highly valued by recruiters in fields including health care, marketing, and sales.

Of course, as retiree organizations such as AARP readily emphasize, foreign language study is an attractive way to spend one's later years productively. Besides providing mental activity more meaningful than playing bingo, it opens doors to friendship and romance, group camaraderie, and even exotic travel through language immersion programs. As Tanya Mohn reported in her *New York Times* article "Learning a New Language on Location," "Americans are not known for their facility with foreign languages, and learning gets more difficult as people age. But that has not stopped 60-, 70- and 80-somethings from heading to senior-friendly . . . classes to tackle verb conjugations and the nuances of idioms—in places like the Tuscan hills and beach towns of Costa Rica."

Learning a foreign language isn't only a gateway to career and social opportunities, but scientific evidence also points to cognitive benefits. A variety of studies have found that bilingual children have better ability to control their attention than their monolingual peers, as well as more effective problem-solving skills. Apparently, there are payoffs related to decision making too. In a well-publicized study, Dr. Boaz Keysar and colleagues at the University of Chicago found that bilingual college students in several countries made better, less-risky decisions when using their second rather than primary language. In the researchers' view, this surprising finding—which they dubbed "the foreign-language effect"—indicates that we think more objectively with a secondary language, perhaps because a different part of the brain is involved than with our original tongue.

New Language, New World

Every language has a culture behind it, so decide which foreign country most intrigues you—whether through the arts, cuisine, literature, or scenery. It's not necessary to have already visited, for you can acquire language proficiency as an "armchair traveler." To strengthen your motivation, join a class rather than study alone and set a reasonable study schedule. From YouTube videos to radio stations and language-partner websites, the Internet offers many resources.

27

LIFE METAPHORS

• • ● • •

IN THREE WORDS or less, what's your view of human existence? Is it akin to war, a game of luck, or strategy, like chess? How about a journey or a mystery tale? Or is it something more fun—like a dance, a party, or a day at the beach? Those are a few of the popular metaphors that people embrace around the world today. Most likely, you also have a favorite one for human nature and personality: Are we essentially machines, flowering plants, trees that grow from tiny seeds, or something else entirely? And what's your metaphor for love relationships: a glorious duet, a joint adventure, a stormy sea? Psychologists increasingly believe that your answers to these questions impact your decision making and actions in daily life.

Essentially, every psychological theory is based on an underlying metaphor. During much of Sigmund Freud's life, the dominant technology was steam power. It was as omnipresent a century ago as computers are for us today. Not surprisingly, Freud chose the steam engine metaphor to describe what he called the "apparatus" of the human mind—in which "psychic energy" flows in a "psychodynamic" system and can neither be created nor destroyed. When humanistic psychology arose in the United States after World War II, innovators Carl Rogers and Abraham Maslow deliberately sought new metaphors. Rogers compared us to flowering plants that require the psychological equivalents of air, soil, and sunlight to grow fully, and Maslow compared us to magnificent trees that arise from tiny acorns. Later, with the growth of computer technology, some psychologists advocated the computer metaphor: human beings are essentially complex information-processing or cybersystems.

Though metaphors for human nature come and go with regularity, it was Alfred Adler who first argued, in the 1930s, that everyone has a particular metaphor for dealing with life. In Adler's view, this *life plan* (as he called it) starts in our childhood and is firmly in place by the age of six. It represents our particular way of navigating life's uncertainties. Where does it originate? For Adlerians, our life plan comes from our inborn physical and mental strengths, and from our early experiences. Therapists and coaches now increasingly focus on the root metaphors that people use to describe their personal lives and relationships.

Interest today in metaphors is also surging in fields ranging from education to business. Drs. George Lakoff and Mark Johnson declared in their groundbreaking book *Metaphors We Live By*: "Metaphors are not mere poetical or rhetorical embellishments. They affect the ways in which we perceive, think, and act. Reality itself is defined by metaphor."

Over the past few years, I've led research internationally in better understanding life metaphors—and how these vary by such aspects as our age, occupation, and nationality. Generally, our main life metaphor changes as we leave adolescence and experience the joys and challenges of adulthood. It also seems that most people view their life metaphor as strongly influencing their daily decision making, long-range plans, and happiness. As you might guess, those who enjoy their work or who aspire to leadership express metaphors that are optimistic, active, and individualistic rather than gloomy, passive, or impersonal. So what's yours?

Sharpen Your View of Life

Take a few minutes and complete this phrase:
Life is like a _____.
What does your answer reveal about your outlook? How does it influence your goals? Since when have you favored this particular metaphor, and why? And, if you'd like to experience greater day-to-day happiness, what other possible metaphors beckon to you?

28

MENtORINg

· • ● •·

"TELL ME AND I forget, teach me and I may remember, involve me and I learn," asserted the Chinese philosopher Xun Kuang. Though composed more than two millennia ago in a vastly different milieu, his message rings true today. Although career counselors have focused mainly on helping young adults to be successful mentees, positive psychology has shown sizable benefits for mentors as well. Especially for men and women in midlife and beyond, the mentoring relationship appears to be a valuable component of meaningful living—certainly worth self-investment of both time and energy.

In psychological terms, mentoring is based on psychoanalyst Erik Erikson's concept of *generativity*, first advanced in *Childhood and Society* in 1950. In this landmark book, Erikson presented eight stages of human development from infancy through old age; each presented a specific task or challenge for growth. He associated midlife—the long seventh stage—with that of generativity: concern and guidance of future generations. Erikson saw parenthood as the chief arena of generativity for most adults. Yet he insightfully argued that not all parents devote their generative energies to their own children, and that generativity is eminently possible without parenthood. The key issue is supportive involvement with younger persons for societal benefit.

The topics of midlife and midlife crisis later gained popular appeal through best-sellers and Hollywood movies—and generated new research. Dr. John Kotre, a former Jesuit seminarian long affiliated with the University of Michigan at Ann Arbor, amplified Erikson's work by identifying four types of generativity. These encompass: (1) the *biological*, involving begetting, bearing, and nursing one's infant; (2) the *parental*, concerned with child discipline and the transmission of family traditions; (3) the *technical*, consumed with teaching practical skills; and (4) the *cultural*, focusing on transmitting values, such as autonomy or religiosity, prized by the particular culture.

More recently, Dr. Dan McAdams at Northwestern University and his colleagues have been investigating why middle-aged people differ from one another in their degree of generativity. While some men and women eagerly nurture younger persons—whether informally or organizationally—others are indifferent or even hostile to mentoring. They have minimal interest in getting involved with youthful learners or career fledglings.

What accounts for such striking differences? It has a lot to do with our role models as we grow into adulthood. If we're lucky enough to have socially involved parents, as well as inspiring teachers and mentors, then we're more likely to embrace generativity in our own lives. Not surprisingly, people with high generativity are more involved in civic, political, and religious activities. As parents, they're also more likely to emphasize the importance of imparting values and wisdom as part of their responsibility—and they're also happier than their more aloof contemporaries. All in all, quite a good combination!

Share Your Mastery

To begin mentoring, it's important to have a positive attitude. But it's also helpful to follow these guidelines to maximize your effectiveness.

1) Choose an activity that reflects your personal interests. This will minimize burnout.

2) Be realistic. No relationship is perfect, so expect occasional snags.

3) To best promote your mentee's growth, encourage decision making rather than dependence.

4) Be an active listener. Allow your mentee to offer fresh ideas and methods in your work together. You'll both benefit.

29

MINDFULNESS

· · ● · ·

"THE WORLD IS full of obvious things which nobody by any chance ever observes," said Arthur Conan Doyle through his most famous literary creation, Sherlock Holmes. Of course, Sherlock was commenting wryly from his perspective as Victorian England's greatest crime detective. Yet the words are eminently relevant to today's growing interest in *mindfulness* as an important facet of psychological well-being. Indeed, mindfulness is proving a highly relevant trait for enhancing romance and friendship, work productivity, and even physical health.

Among the leading psychologists to emphasize the importance of mindfulness is Dr. Ellen Langer. A prolific Harvard researcher for over thirty years,

she first became interested in the topic while studying how people unconsciously process information.
"[Cognitive experts] in the field were concerned with
the different ways people think," Langer recalled in a
2010 interview in *Harvard Magazine*, "and I questioned
whether, and on which occasions, we might not be
thinking at all." Dr. Langer's ensuing studies generated
the concept of *mindlessness*, which, she explains, "is
not the same thing as stupidity. . . . You're on automatic
pilot . . . relying on the distinctions and categories that
you drew in the past, so the past is over-determining
the present. You're trapped in a single perspective."
In a variety of studies, she and her colleagues found
that mindfulness was vital for optimal cognitive
functioning.

During the same time, in the late 1970s, cardiolo-
gist Herbert Benson, also at Harvard, and psychologist
Jon Kabat-Zinn at the University of Massachusetts
Medical School both began advocating the health
benefits of mindful meditation. In contrast, Dr. Langer
and her exponents view mindfulness more as an overall attitude toward life than a particular relaxation

or breathing technique. For this reason, they argue that methods for enhancing moment-to-moment awareness of what's happening around us are less crucial than an inner commitment to focusing on the present—such as involving family members, friends, coworkers, and others in our daily interactions.

All too often, Langer maintains, we erroneously see others not as they are *right now* in our lives, but as they were some time in the past. "Virtually all of us, almost all the time, are not there," she said in one of her many public lectures. And this matters "because all of our suffering—personal, interpersonal, societal—is a function, directly or indirectly, of this mindlessness." According to Dr. Langer's empirical scale, mindfulness in daily life comprises four separate aspects: novelty seeking, novelty producing, flexibility, and engagement. In a study led by Dr. Leslie Burpee at Harvard University, marital satisfaction for both men and women was significantly linked to mindfulness—and this psychological trait was more important than any other for such happiness, even more so than perceived similarity between spouses.

In other words, those who were mentally engaged, open to new experiences, and aware of new contexts enjoyed more satisfying, fulfilling relations. When it comes to romance, it seems, never opt for autopilot.

Tune into the Now

Becoming more mindful isn't something you can accomplish overnight. Two classic methods from Gestalt Therapy—developed by Drs. Frederick Perls and Ralph Hefferline with writer Paul Goodman—are easy enough. With the first, set a timer daily for a specific period of time, say ten minutes, and then sit quietly and close your eyes. Focus your attention solely on your body. Tune out everything else, including thoughts. For the second, follow the same procedure but focus wholly on your external environment, such as sounds or odors. For both activities, you may increase your allotted time as your prowess improves.

MORAL ELATION

· · ● · ·

DID YOU KNOW that Thomas Jefferson helped to create a new specialty in positive psychology? Surprisingly, America's third president has given rise to the study of *elation*—our uplifting feeling when witnessing an act of goodness. Several years ago, Dr. Jonathan Haidt of New York University found this observation by Jefferson to be provocative: "When any act of charity or gratitude is presented either to our sight or imagination, we are deeply impressed with its beauty—and feel a strong desire . . . of doing charitable acts also." An interesting thought, but was it scientifically true?

A series of experiments by Haidt and his international colleagues revealed the answer is a definite yes. Both subjectively, in terms of feelings, and also with regard to objective consequences, elevation (as his team also calls it) proved to be a real emotional state—distinct from momentary happiness. Specifically, elevation was associated specifically with "feeling moved and uplifted, having a warm feeling in the chest, and wanting to become a better person . . . and to help others."

Intriguingly, experimental research has shown that inspiring movies, documentary or fictional, can also evoke moral elation. This finding is consistent with the therapeutic work of mental health professionals. For example, when I recently posted an Internet query on the use of film in this context, colleagues around the world eagerly reported how particular movies catalyzed emotional uplift among their clients. These included epic biographies such as *Gandhi* and *Schindler's List*, as well as "smaller" films, such as *The Book Thief* and *Groundhog Day.* My related query on an alumni website concerning personal uplift from movies evoked many heartfelt replies, including these: "After seven years in media sales, I was looking for new challenges. Then I saw *Stand and Deliver* about educator Jaime

Escalante. . . . It was the most influential factor in my decision to teach on both college and high school levels." And: "I remember seeing *12 Angry Men* [a drama about a deadlocked jury on a murder case] and thinking that one person—acting against the odds—can make a difference."

Among today's leading psychologists in studying such intriguing phenomena is Dr. Ryan Niemiec of Xavier University in Cincinnati, Ohio. In his view, cinematic elevation may manifest in several possible ways after one views an inspiring movie character or theme. For example, we may become motivated to copy the protagonist's core strengths to improve ourselves or others. Thus, *The Shawshank Redemption* leads some viewers to practice more hope and perseverance in their own lives. Others, after watching a movie like *The Artist*, decide to express a strength or virtue different from what was portrayed—such as gratitude for life rather than zest. And still others become motivated to "do good" or improve themselves through a changed outlook. From my professional experience, films often mentioned in this context include *As Good as It Gets*, *Finding Forrester*, and director Frank Capra's classic *It's a Wonderful Life*.

The list of inspiring movies is long, and that's surely an encouraging thing.

Inspiration for Moral Elation

. . . .

Because elation spurs good deeds as well as personal happiness, it's useful to recall acts of kindness, courage, or altruism that you've witnessed. When was the last time in daily life that you saw someone behaving courageously or altruistically? How did it make you feel? Could you "pass it on" somehow to others? As for movies, which ones have inspired you—even if briefly—to be a better person? Or a video clip, perhaps? Which would you recommend to a teenager needing an uplift about human nature, and why?

NOSTALGIA

· · ● · ·

DO YOU INDULGE in sentimental memories? Do you enjoy perusing photo collections or listening to "oldies" songs on the radio or YouTube, or other popular media? If so, don't feel embarrassed—for social scientists now say that nostalgia isn't only harmless but actually beneficial for our well-being. Indeed, the more emotionally healthy we are, the likelier we are to feel sentimental easily.

It certainly wasn't always this way. The word *nostalgia* comes from ancient Greek, combining *nostos* ("homecoming") and *algos* ("pain, suffering, or grief"). The word was created back in 1688 by a Swiss physician named Johannes Hofer, who discussed it in a medical treatise. He used nostalgia to describe the severe emotional distress of Swiss soldiers stationed far from home—whose symptoms included sadness, diminished senses, and physical weakness.

For centuries afterward, nostalgia had a medical—and basically abnormal—connotation linked to home-sickness. For a while, some medical researchers even suggested that it was peculiar to Swiss people. Then, in the 1950s, experts began changing their view. They no longer saw nostalgia as a type of homesickness but instead as a pleasant self-indulgence about the past. Undoubtedly, this shift related to the enormous impact of TV, whose popular shows like *Death Valley Days*, *Gunsmoke*, and *Wagon Train* celebrated the American Old West and Frontier. Other shows, like *Lassie*, cast a warm glow on the traditional American farm. It's no surprise that baby boomers—raised on such entertaining fare—were the first generation to grow up with nostalgia as a positive feature.

Today, positive psychology has shed increasing light on the role of nostalgia in our lives. What do we know? First, that most people become nostalgic mainly about their teenage and young adult years, rather than their childhood. Perhaps it's because we fondly recall our first, awakening sense of freedom and life's great possibilities.

We also know that nostalgic moods are often triggered by our senses—especially involving songs and odors. Intriguingly, American regional differences seem to exist: In *Advances in Consumer Research*, Dr. Alan Hirsch reported that for East Coast people, the fragrance of flowers is most likely to evoke a happy childhood memory, whereas Southerners react more to fresh country air. For Midwesterners, it's the smell of farm animals, and for West Coasters, it's the aroma of meat cooking outdoors. Vintage cars and reminiscing about big-league sports often put men in nostalgic moods, whereas women react more to mementos associated with particular events involving family or friends. For many people, the major holidays trigger happy memories.

More important, nostalgia has qualities that benefit our mental health. An international team of researchers led by Dr. Xinyue Zhou in China found that nostalgia helped people to feel more connected with family and friends, thereby reducing feelings of loneliness. These findings affirmed an earlier study led by Dr. Tim Wildschut at the University of Southampton in England. Both researchers contend that people with high resilience—the ability to bounce back quickly from stress—are skillful in using nostalgia to put themselves in a happy mood.

Of course, it probably isn't healthy to overindulge in nostalgia. Focusing too much on past memories can prevent us from living fully in the present, and from strengthening current relationships. But in moderation, nostalgia can wonderfully enhance our sense of closeness to others.

Music to Remember

Name three songs that put you in a nostalgic mood. For each one, what's your strongest memory? Describe the circumstances and people who were with you. How can you build on these memories for greater happiness in your life?

32

OVERCOMING REGRETS

· · ● · ·

DO YOU HAVE any regrets in life? Seemingly, everyone does—and it's probably been this way since recorded history. The ancient Israelites regretted having fled Egypt as slaves and blamed Moses for their desert malaise. The American revolutionary spy Nathan Hale famously regretted "having but one life to give" for his new nation. And the most acclaimed business leader of our time, Steve Jobs, regretted in a final interview that he had not been closer to his four children.

Surprisingly, this topic has only recently begun to receive scientific attention. A century ago, Sigmund Freud uncovered plenty of guilt in his middle-class Viennese patients—and linked it to suppressed sexual thoughts. Today, psychologists view regret as a different, broader phenomenon. Certainly, we can have regrets without feeling guilty about our thoughts or actions. Psychological research is now converging on the notion that *what* we regret, how *often* we do so, and with what *intensity* all make a difference. These findings make intuitive sense if regret is as universal as it seems— for not everyone is fixated on past mistakes or missed opportunities in life, while some people can't ever seem to let go.

What has positive psychology discovered with regard to regret? Let's take a quick look.

First, there's a big distinction between our regrets over *actions* versus our regrets over *inactions*. Regrets over actions seem to elicit mainly "hot" emotions such as anger ("How could I have been so stupid as to buy that car!"). Regrets over inactions typically elicit feelings of wistfulness ("What if I had moved to London with Kathy that summer instead of staying in Cleveland?") or despair ("Why didn't I go to law school when I had the chance? I've wasted my life selling life insurance.").

Research shows, too, that people experience more regret in the short term over their actions, but, as they age, this attitude reverses.

In other words, you're likely to find lots of folks in their twenties or thirties whose chief regrets are about foolish things they've done. In contrast, those in midlife and beyond are likelier to voice regrets on what they *didn't* do—and those regrets may be more painful to bear.

What's absolutely clear is that severe regret is bad for our mental and even physical health. Research led by Dr. Isabelle Bauer at Sunnybrook Health Sciences Centre in Toronto found that people who compared themselves to successful friends and neighbors had more frequent colds than those who compared themselves to those whom they considered worse off. A study by Dr. Carsten Wrosch at Concordia University in Montreal linked severe regrets among the elderly to increased sleep difficulties, cortisol imbalance, and diminished feelings of happiness.

Can we learn to minimize our regrets and thereby improve our emotional well-being? It definitely seems so. Experimental research suggests that keeping a journal—especially to write about a painful personal experience—helps us to process the event and let it go. Perhaps the British writer Katherine Mansfield said it best when she mused, "Regret is an appalling waste of energy. . . . You can't get it into shape; you can't build on it. It's only good for wallowing."

The Past Is Past

Think of a regret of commission, and give yourself adequate time to write about it fully. Then let your emotional attachment go. For a persistent regret of omission, it's useful to make a thorough "reality check." That is, would things really have changed much in your life if you had done that, or are you just fantasizing a perfect scenario in our imperfect world, to little or no benefit?

33

PEAK
EXPERIENCES

· · ● · ·

"WHAT CAN YOU do if you're thirty and, turning
the corner of your own street, you are overcome, suddenly, by a feeling of bliss—absolute bliss—as though
you'd suddenly swallowed a bright piece of that late
afternoon?" asked Katherine Mansfield in her story
Bliss. The British writer was herself age thirty at the
time, and, though she lived only four more years, her
life was vibrant with dazzling moments. It's likely that
Mansfield would have appreciated Abraham Maslow's
scientific quest to uncover their value for our emotional,
and possibly even physical, well-being.

Maslow called these dazzling moments *peak experiences*. They emerged from his studies, beginning in
the mid-1940s, of emotionally healthy, high-achieving

adults—whom he would later call "self-actualized."
As a young Brooklyn College professor, he recognized
that his research was revolutionary—for psychology
until then had focused almost exclusively on either
mentally ill or average people. As Maslow later wrote,
"If we want to know how fast a human being can run,
then it is no use to average out the speed of a 'good
sample' of the population. It is far better to collect
Olympic gold medal winners and see how well they
can do."

In interviewing high achievers, Maslow discovered that they reported frequent moments of great joy
and fulfillment in everyday life. Even more intriguingly, the words they used to describe such moments
often resembled the accounts of history's great mystics
and sages. Having long been skeptical about religious
dogma, Maslow found these results perplexing, but he
was never one ignore to scientific evidence. Slowly, he
amassed data from biographies, detailed interviews,
and surveys of college students until ready to share his
findings with the scientific world. His paper, presented
at the American Psychological Association convention

in 1956, specified the link between "the highest reaches of human nature" and peak experiences—and described nearly twenty features of such exalted moments. These included great happiness, feelings of awe, temporary disorientation with regard to time and space, and a complete loss of fear and defense before the grandeur of the universe.

Perhaps composing the most important aspect of his paper, Maslow noted that peak experiences often leave profound, transformative effects in their wake. Generally, he commented, "The person is more apt to feel that life . . . is worthwhile, even if it is usually drab, pedestrian, painful, or ungratifying, since beauty, truth, and meaningfulness have been demonstrated . . . to exist." In later years, Maslow speculated that many people suffering from emotional disorders such as depression, alcoholism, and drug abuse were "starving" for such wondrous moments. Thus, in his influential book *Religions, Values, and Peak-Experiences*, he poetically asserted, "The power of the peak-experience could permanently affect [one's] attitude toward life. A single glimpse of heaven is enough to confirm its existence, even if it is never experienced again."

During the past decade, my colleagues and I have explored youthful and midlife peak experiences around the globe. In every country and region—from Brazil and Chile to Hong Kong and Japan—those involving interpersonal joy are predominant. To a lesser extent, peaks are linked to events involving aesthetic delight, nature, external achievement, religious activity, and skill mastery.

Heights of Happiness

Describe a peak experience in your life—preferably one that occurred within the past year. Who was with you at the time, or were you alone? What triggered this moment of great happiness? What impact did it subsequently have on your view of life? What can you do to generate more wonderful, uplifting experiences?

34

PETS

· · ● · ·

ARE YOU A dog or cat lover, or happily drawn instead to birds or fish? How about animals such as ferrets, hamsters, rabbits, or snakes? The list of domestic animal possibilities is long, and growing. The majority of all U.S. households own a pet, and, in many homes, pets are loved as family members. From Lassie and Rin Tin Tin to Cheetah and Flipper, animals are treasured in popular culture. But all this is certainly not a new phenomenon. More than 2,500 years ago, Homer's *Odyssey* featured Argos—among the first dogs ever named in Western literature. He was also the most faithful of them all, waiting twenty years for Odysseus to return—and the only creature, human or animal, to recognize him when he finally arrived.

Sigmund Freud and his daughter Dr. Anna Freud kept dogs, and Carl Jung walked a small pig on a leash. But today, the psychological study of pet ownership is only now gaining momentum. Early researchers included Dr. James Bossard, who during World War II authored the upbeat article "The Mental Hygiene of Owning a Dog," and Dr. Boris Levinson, credited as the founder of animal-assisted therapy (AAT) in the 1960s. His seminal article, "The Dog as a 'Co-Therapist,'" described how his dog, Jingles, helped treat a socially withdrawn boy. In follow-up work, Levinson emphasized the therapeutic value of pets for emotionally distressed children—and the field slowly expanded to include students with cognitive disabilities such as autism, as well as adults with HIV, traumatic brain injury, dementia, and other major health problems. Professionals also began reporting anecdotally that pets contribute broadly to human happiness and wellness, and subsequent scientific studies have revealed such benefits as lower blood pressure, less loneliness, and higher self-esteem.

Precisely how pet ownership helps us psychologically remains a puzzle. However, a recent study in

Science gives a clue. A team of Japanese researchers found that dogs that gazed for a long time at their owners had elevated levels of oxytocin—the brain's "pleasure hormone" associated with attachment. After receiving those gazes, the owners' oxytocin increased too. When researchers gave dogs extra oxytocin via a nasal spray, the females gazed at their owners even longer—which, in turn, amplified the owners' levels. As Dr. Evan Maclean, codirector of Duke University's Canine Cognition Center, commented on this study, "Maybe dogs gaze at you because it feels good. Maybe they're hugging you with their eyes."

Currently, the field is led by two professional bodies. In the U.S., the former Delta Foundation—now known as Pet Partners—was organized in 1977 by a visionary group of physicians and veterinarians. Its achievements include the establishment of the National Service Dog Center, which focuses on advocacy and outreach for disabled people seeking a service dog trainer. The International Society for Animal-Assisted Therapy was founded in Zurich, Switzerland, in 2006. Led by researchers in psychiatry and veterinary medicine, its goal is to create high global standards for animal-assisted therapy, education, and related activities.

Animal Appreciation

· · · · · · · · · · · · · ·

If you have a pet, write about its effect on your daily well-being. How and when did it come into your life? What aspects of your pet do you most enjoy, and why? If you don't have a pet, volunteer at an animal shelter. You can also attend a local pet adoption event—typically a festive, weekend effort in which shelter and rescue groups seek homes for cats, dogs, rabbits, or other animals without owners.

PHOTOGRAPHY

· · • · ·

IS PHOTOGRAPHY JUST a hobby—or something more vital for personal well-being, a way toward self-realization? This intriguing question, increasingly raised by positive psychology today, has also caught Hollywood's attention. As depicted in a recent version of *The Secret Life of Walter Mitty*, Sean O'Connell (played by Sean Penn) is a famous, adventurous photojournalist—and hero to his nerdy, office-bound assistant, Walter. After years of communicating only by mail, they finally meet on a Himalayan mountaintop. There, Walter—a perpetual daydreamer—is transformed by Sean's message as he photographs a ghostly snow leopard: Be fully in the moment, here and now.

This concept of "mindful photography," as it's popularly known, originated with Minor White, who studied during the 1940s with such luminaries as Alfred Stieglitz, Ansel Adams, and Edward Weston. White was especially influenced by Stieglitz's notion of "the equivalent"—in which a photographic image becomes a visual metaphor for a state of being. Later, at MIT, after delving into Zen Buddhism, White taught the importance of meditation and mindfulness for photography, and as a way of life. "Be still with your-self until the object of your attention affirms your presence," he advised. More broadly, he observed, "Innocence of eye has a quality of its own. It means to see as a child sees, with freshness and an even deeper sense of wonder."

Though systematic research remains scanty, health professionals are increasingly using photography for its emotional benefits. In 2008, the First International Conference on Phototherapy and Therapeutic Photog-raphy took place in Finland—with presentations by art therapists, psychologists, and social workers. Among its leaders was Judy Weiser, whose book *Phototherapy Techniques* gave methods for using personal snapshots, family albums, and photos taken by others to spur self-reflection and improve therapeutic communication. Originally an offshoot of art therapy, the wider use of photography to enhance well-being is gaining popularity through adult classes and workshops. Such programs emphasize how photos can serve as a visual diary for self-insight, enhance positive memories, foster creativity, and strengthen connections with others.

Mindful photography is also being used in the classroom. In a project designed to teach children the concept of well-being, Drs. Saoirse Gabhainn and Jane Sixsmith at the National University of Ireland instructed a group of eight- to twelve-year-olds to take photos of "things they liked," while a follow-up group organized these into categories such as "people I love the most," "food and drink," and "animals/pets." According to the researchers, photography proved an effective instructional tool on the concept of well-being. Dr. Anne Kellock, at Sheffield Hallam University in England, found that participatory photo taking among poor, New Zealand Maori eight- to ten-year-olds helped them identify important aspects of their lives.

Psychologists active in this field are using photography with older students too. In a recent handbook for college instructors, Drs. Jaime Kurtz of James Madison University in Virginia and Sonja Lyubomirsky at the University of California at Riverside recommended that students take photos of everyday things that give them joy and then, as a group, discuss their collective output.

continued ➥

Imaging the Moment

· · · · · · · · · · · · ·

Choose a theme—such as animals, architecture, or people—and strive for unique images while photo taking. To maximize your mindfulness, follow these tips:

* Shooting color will align your eye and mind, so look for something colorful, then get in close.

* Take photos of textures, which are always affected by light quality. Imagine you're touching what you see.

* When photographing people, start with those you know well. Be patient. Eventually they'll stop straining to look "good," and you'll get better pictures of their true presence in the moment.

36

POETRY

· · ● · ·

"POETRY LIFTS THE veil from the hidden beauty of the world," exulted Percy Shelley, "and makes familiar objects be as if they were not familiar." The great nineteenth-century poet intimately knew his craft's power to uplift the mind—a connection recognized for millennia. For example, the influential Roman physician Soranus prescribed poetry and drama for patients—tragedy for those who were manic and comedy for ones who were depressed.

Though early founders of psychotherapy such as Sigmund Freud and Carl Jung praised the insights of poets, the specialty known as *poetry therapy* emerged relatively recently. In 1976, Dr. Arthur Lerner authored *Poetry in the Therapeutic Experience* and founded the

Poetry Therapy Institute in Los Angeles. Four years later, a national convocation involving Dr. Lerner and colleagues led to the establishment of the National Association for Poetry Therapy—the field's major professional organization and sponsor of the *Journal of Poetry Therapy.*

Today, poetry is increasingly used in counseling, psychotherapy, and other clinical settings. Researchers are also gaining scientific evidence regarding its effectiveness. Drs. Beth Boone and Linda Castillo at Texas A & M University in 2008 found that poetry therapy helped reduce post-traumatic stress disorder (PTSD) symptoms among domestic violence counselors. Those who responded in writing to specific, emotionally charged poems relevant to domestic violence showed lower PTSD than control-group peers who didn't participate. More recently, Dr. Grace Brillantes-Evangelista of Miriam College in the Philippines found that poetry therapy was effective in reducing depression among adolescents with a history of abuse. Poetry therapy has also been empirically validated in health fields ranging from palliative care to psychotherapy.

In view of such findings, it's not surprising that the Yale School of Medicine since 2011 has sponsored a poetry-writing contest for its students. More than 450 poems have been submitted on a variety of themes ranging from the mythic to the mundane, and from aphasia to surgery. Though such illustrious writers as John Keats, Walker Percy, and William Carlos Williams were all trained as physicians, the contest's goal isn't to produce literary icons. Rather, as Dr. Timothy Duffy of Yale Medical School noted, "Poetry opens our minds to asking patients the right questions, while helping us address the emotional demands of doctoring, especially in the formative years." Consistent with this view, the school is developing a required literary reading list for students that includes poetry.

In her final lecture as United States Poet Laureate, Natasha Trethewey in 2012 recounted the inspirational role of poetry in her childhood and its healing power when, as a teenager, she struggled to cope with her mother's violent death. She ended her speech before the Library of Congress with these inspiring words: "Poetry is the . . . sacred language that allows us to connect across time and space, across all the things . . . that separate us and destroy us. It evokes in us 'the better angels of our nature,' . . . our . . . emotional knowledge, our empathic understanding. . . . "

Find Your Inner Poet
. . . .

It's probably been a long time since you've written a poem. Choose a topic that's person- ally meaningful. Though some poets prefer to let their words flow spontaneously, it's easier if you first decide on the voice (first, second, or third person) and style (such as rhyming or free verse). Then write! Reread and edit aloud. Sharing is optional; what matters is finding your voice from life experience.

37

POWER NAPPING

• • ● • •

LONG BEFORE THE rise of Silicon Valley's high-powered techies, Thomas Edison zealously promoted his reputation as a tireless visionary. Consistent with his famous maxim that "Genius is ninety-nine percent perspiration, one percent inspiration," he boasted of sleeping only three or four hours nightly—and laboring for seventy-two hours straight at times. But the truth is more complex. One day, his friend Henry Ford came to visit Edison at his lab—and his assistant stopped him from entering because the famed inventor was snoozing. "But I thought Edison didn't sleep very much," Ford snorted. To which the assistant replied, "He doesn't sleep very much; he just naps a lot."

Was Edison secretly on to something? How about Albert Einstein, who perfected his own napping routine? Sitting in his favorite armchair, Einstein would hold a pencil or spoon in hand—and placing a plate below him, fade to the Land of Nod. When his resting hand released the object to the floor, Einstein would instantly awaken from the resulting clatter. His micronaps lasted only a minute or two, but the world's best-known physicist reported their effectiveness. The artist Salvador Dalí initiated a similar technique with a key as his wake-up object. In the realm of politics, Winston Churchill was renowned for his midafternoon siestas—and invented the term *power nap* to describe their efficacy.

Over the past decade, scientific research has confirmed that napping carries substantial mental and physical benefits, starting at infancy. Dr. Rebecca Gómez and her colleagues at the University of Arizona found naps improved abstract language learning in toddlers. As Drs. Amber Tietzel and Leon Lack at Australia's Flinders University reported, young adults who nap for as little as ten minutes reap benefits in both alertness and cognitive performance compared with non-nappers—but ultra-brief naps of thirty and ninety seconds proved ineffective. In a study by Dr. Matthew Walker and colleagues at the University of California at Berkeley, healthy young adults who napped midday for ninety minutes did better on a variety of learning tasks than a napless control group. In the researchers' view, napping has an important restorative function for the hippocampus—the brain's region active in forming new memories. As Walker commented, "It's as though the email box in your hippocampus is full, and, until you sleep and clear those out, you're not going to receive any more mail. It's just going to bounce until you sleep and move it into another folder." Other researchers believe that napping enhances creativity by activating the hypnagogic state—that brief period, often filled with vivid imagery, right before we enter sleep.

Increasingly, corporate America is recognizing that afternoon snoozes improve employee productivity. Among the first such companies was Google, which has promoted napping via "energy pods"—reclining chairs inside a large bubble, usually with built-in soothing music and an alarm that awakens employees by vibration and lights. Nap rooms—or "rejuvenation centers," as they're euphemistically called—are especially popular in the tech industry, where developers—like Edison's engineers a century ago—often toil long hours. Perhaps somewhere among his vast papers lies the "energy pod" prototype.

Midday Recharge

A power nap can't replace all your lost sleep, but it can certainly help. Most people get sleepy in the midafternoon, so experts advise that you rest in a quiet, cool dark room at that time and limit your nap to twenty or thirty minutes. Keep a notepad nearby, as you may get valuable ideas during the hypnagogic state.

38

PRAYER

· · ● · ·

"I PRAY WHENEVER I'm in trouble," related Isaac Bashevis Singer, the Nobel Prize-winning Yiddish writer, "And because I'm always in trouble, I pray almost constantly." With his mischievous sense of humor, Singer enjoyed jousting with reporters skeptical of his spiritual outlook. Could such a brilliant, insightful storyteller really believe in a transcendent world—or was it all just a put-on? In fact, Singer, who was raised in a venerable Polish rabbinic family steeped in Kabbalah, was sincere. In his view, prayer is central to impassioned living—whether in preindustrial Europe or the post-Holocaust world.

Though long ignored by later researchers, prayer was a vital topic of well-being for William James, founder of American psychology. In his *Varieties of Religious Experience*—presented as lectures at the University of Edinburgh from 1901 to 1902—he described prayer as "the very soul and essence of religion." Conceding that many colleagues dismissed the subject as unscientific, James nonetheless asserted, "It may well prove that . . . prayer is subjective exclusively . . . but through [it], religion insists, things which cannot be realized in any other manner come about." Recounting prayerful accounts in Christianity, Islam, and Judaism, James poetically noted: "It is as if all doors were opened, and all paths freshly smoothed. We meet a new world. . . . "

Though scientific study of prayer languished for a century, the advent of positive psychology has generated new attention. The focus has been on whether prayer fosters desirable emotions, and if so, how? Despite the relative infancy of this research, some consistent findings are already emerging. Let's have a quick look.

First, as James recognized long ago, prayers come in different forms—and not all exert the same psychological impact. Brandon Whittington and Dr. Steven Scher of Eastern Illinois University identified six types of prayer, encompassing:

1. *adoration*, or worshipping God without any reference to one's needs or desires

2. *thanksgiving*, or expressing gratitude to God, usually made in reference to one's uplifting life experiences

3. *petitionary* prayers, requests for divine intervention to aid oneself or others

4. *confession*, involving one's admission of misdeeds and request for God's forgiveness

5. prayers of *reception*, comprising a contemplative openness to divine guidance

6. *obligatory* prayers, mainly ritualistic and repeated at fixed worship times

As you might expect, prayers of thanksgiving are psychologically beneficial, for they strengthen our sense of gratitude—a key emotion for personal well-being. Prayers involving adoration or reception produce payoffs in strengthening optimism, self-esteem, and meaning in life. In contrast, confessional prayer is linked to *worse* functioning on such measures. Though firm conclusions are elusive, it seems better to diminish our ego while praying than amplify it. In an intriguing study by Dr. Nathaniel Lambert at Florida State University and his colleagues, men and women who privately made a single prayer concerning their romantic partner's well-being significantly increased their forgiveness for the partner's misdeeds, as compared with a control group. A follow-up study revealed that month-long daily praying for a close friend boosted selfless concern for others generally. In short, prayer's a good way to let go of resentment and see the world in a more positive light.

Conversing with the Infinite

Whether you're accustomed to praying or new to the practice, choose two people with whom you're close and pray for their well-being. To center yourself, close your eyes, take a few relaxing breaths, and then visualize your loved ones surrounded by light. You may wish to picture them smiling or laughing. Whether using your own heartfelt words or those linked to a particular faith tradition, you'll feel happier as a result.

RESTORATIVE NATURE

"EVERYBODY NEEDS BEAUTY ... [places] where nature may heal and cheer," mused America's famous naturalist John Muir, "and give strength to the body and soul alike." An ardent conservationist who inspired President Theodore Roosevelt and Congress to create the national parks system, Muir had a fervent view of nature's beneficial effect upon the human psyche. Now, more than a century after his death in 1914, researchers are increasingly recognizing the accuracy of his insights.

Among the dominant themes in this field is psychological restoration—the sense of renewed vitality, strength, and even hope that immersion in nature may often impart. For nearly twenty-five years, Dr. Terry

Hartig at Uppsala University in Sweden has been at the forefront in studying this topic. An international team under his leadership found a variety of individual benefits in strolling through a nature preserve, as compared with a comparable walk in a city setting—including lower blood pressure and a better mood. More recent efforts have focused on advancing this specialty conceptually, with particular relevance for public health and environmental science. In Hartig's cogent view, it's unrealistic to expect many people to experience wilderness settings. Thus, the challenge for scientists is focus on creating restorative milieus within urban civilization.

Dr. Hartig readily acknowledges that uplifting early life experiences provided an important source of motivation for his professional work. "I spent much time in the woods behind our home in Cascade, Michigan, while growing up," he reminisced, "and I remember those woods fondly as a pleasant place for solitude, as well as a place to retreat with friends. A large section of those woods was cut down to make way for a new road and housing, and I still feel that loss. Later, my first hiking trip in the Sierra Nevada of California also provided inspiration and helped me appreciate more of my own capability to persist with difficult challenges."

Other researchers today, such as Australia's Kathryn Williams and David Harvey, have explored transcendent experiences triggered by nature. Based on the work of theorists including William James, Abraham Maslow, and Mihaly Csikszentmihalyi, they elicited reports of exalted moments in forest settings. Generally, these occurred when people were most familiar and relaxed with their natural milieu, and, in a finding surprising to the researchers—rarely when physically active, as when hiking.

There's also evidence that nature is not only restorative for us emotionally, but cognitively beneficial too. Even more intriguing, it may not actually be necessary to immerse in nature to gain this advantage. Dr. Rita Berto of the University of Padua in Italy found, in an influential study, that college students exposed to nature photos recovered more quickly from a tiring computer task than those shown urban scenes or geometric patterns. Later, Dr. Marc Berman and his colleagues at the University of Michigan at Ann Arbor found that college students exposed to nature photos did better on an attentional task than peers presented with urban photos. Such studies have given rise to a new psychological approach called Attention Restoration Theory (ART), emphasizing the cognitive payoff for nature experiences.

Self-Healing Through Nature

Getting to a wilderness preserve isn't easy, but within access to nearly every city and town are restorative places of nature. Botanical gardens and large parks are especially conducive to improving your physical and emotional well-being. Stroll or cycle depending on the weather and your mood. As much as possible, seek restorative sites you can include in your daily routine.

40

SAVORING

· · ● ··

"THE PASSING MOMENT is all we can be sure of,"
observed the British writer W. Somerset Maugham in
his memoir *The Summing Up.* "It is only common sense
to extract its utmost value from it. The future will one
day be the present and will seem as unimportant as
the present does now." Maugham was well past midlife when he wrote those evocative words in 1938, and
his hard-won insight is central to positive psychology's
concept of *savoring*: recognizing, appreciating, and
enhancing small, happy experiences in daily living.

Among today's leading researchers in this domain
is Dr. Fred Bryant of Chicago's Loyola University. While
growing up, he was influenced by his mother's "natural
gift" (his words) for cherishing little joyful moments—

and later confirmed scientifically that personal well-being involved more than just reducing stress. For the past decade, he and international colleagues have been studying what amplifies joy and, equally important, what weakens or saps it. Their surprising, essential finding is that we often fail to maximize the good things in our lives because we lack the right "strategies"—or worse, choose the wrong ones—for doing so. In other words, we're constantly shortchanging ourselves by unknowingly keeping our joys brief and fleeting—preventing their growth or inadvertently suppressing them inwardly.

Drs. Paul Jose and Bee Lim at New Zealand's Victoria University of Wellington, together with Bryant, in one study asked 101 men and women to keep diaries for thirty days. They recorded "pleasant events" and how much they savored or squelched these occurrences. *Savorers* increased their happiness by stopping to focus on the positive event, telling someone about it, or laughing or even yelling about it in delight. In contrast, the *nonsavorers* dampened their own joy by insisting that they didn't deserve the experience, or complaining that it could have been better or didn't last long enough. In another study, Drs. Daniel Hurley and Paul Kwon at Washington State University found that people undergoing tough times gained bigger boosts from savored moments than people whose lives were packed with positive but unsavored experiences. The researchers concluded that savoring is especially vital for our well-being when we're feeling a lull in uplifting or exhilarating events.

In practical terms, what does this mean? Bryant's recommendations to enhance savoring include:

- Tell your friends about your happy experience—whether an entertaining movie, an excellent restaurant, or a memorable vacation spot. By recounting the event, you strengthen it.

- Take a mental photo of the experience. That is, be consciously aware of what's making you happy and fulfilled, such as a loved one's touch or a friend's laughter.

- Congratulate yourself for an achievement or a well-earned outcome. It'll increase your happiness.

- Sharpen your sensory perceptions. Pay more attention to sounds, colors, fragrances, tastes, and tactile sensations. There's evidence that savoring is strongly influenced by our senses, so don't shut them off.

Revel in Your Senses

To enhance your savoring, choose two activities that you do daily—one indoors and the other outside your home. For example, these can involve showering or eating dinner, cycling or strolling around your neighborhood. At least initially, make these solo endeavors and minimize distractions—so, no cell phone! Now slow yourself down. Concentrate fully on what you're experiencing. Open yourself to all five senses; then pick one sense to guide your awareness. What do you notice? What seems new or different? Feel time expanding and enhancing your well-being.

41

SELF-COMPASSION

· • ● • ·

DO YOU TREAT other people kindly but tend to be too hard on yourself—too self-critical, self-berating? If so, you're certainly not alone; and positive psychology has given increasing attention to the trait known as self-compassion. The ability to treat oneself with caring, concern, and kindness has been the subject of many studies during the past few years, and it appears important throughout our life. Research with young adults shows that self-compassion is linked to higher life satisfaction, optimism, agreeableness, and wisdom. It's also associated with lower anxiety and depression, as well as serving as an important "buffer" when stressful or challenging situations arise.

How about older adults? The evidence is fascinating that those with higher self-compassion accept the travails of aging more acceptingly; by striving to be kindly to themselves, they gain prowess in coping with mental and physical difficulties. Australian psychologists Dr. Wendy Phillips and Susan Ferguson found that among those age sixty-five and older, self-compassion was linked with positive emotions such as excitement and enthusiasm, effective coping, and sense of life meaning. Those with greater self-compassion also scored lower on measures of negative emotions like hostility and shame.

It's hardly surprising that self-compassion is frequently linked to mindfulness, for traditional Buddhist thought has strongly influenced both concepts. Dr. Kristin Neff at the University of Texas in Austin, perhaps the world's leading researcher of self-compassion, has been a strong advocate of Insight Meditation (derived from Theravada Buddhism) since her final year of graduate school nearly twenty years ago. "I was going through a messy divorce," she reminisced in an interview, "and had a lot of stress in my life. I really needed self-compassion to get me through all the emotional turmoil. I was in a Buddhist group, and they talked about mindfulness and compassion.

The self-compassion bit really hit me almost immediately. I just thought, wow, I have the right to compassion like everyone else." Several years later, Dr. Neff received another life jolt when she and her husband learned that their son was autistic. "And again," she recalled, "It just saved me, giving myself the time to deal with my grief. . . . I would just send myself compassion quite intensely. It just saved me, so I know that it works."

Investigators like Dr. Neff are careful to distinguish self-compassion from both self-pity and self-indulgence. In their view, self-pity involves being consumed with one's problems and forgetting that other people struggle too. In contrast, self-compassion means seeing matters realistically—as exactly what they are. It's also a tougher kind of love that rejects momentary pleasure—like eating a pint of ice cream when a low mood hits—in favor of a firmer, more long-term caring for one's health and happiness. And it's also different from self-esteem, especially the extreme of narcissism, for self-compassion is not a way of viewing yourself as more important than others—but as equally deserving of kindness, support, and understanding. And the one who's most influential in treating you that way is yourself.

Befriend Yourself

· · · · · · · · · · · ·

To foster greater self-compassion, keep a journal for a week. Each day, recount an event in which you acted or spoke negatively, for example, if you snapped at a family member—and which you now regret in hindsight. After your description, write some kindly, reassuring words of comfort toward yourself, such as "It's okay. We all make mistakes. You'll do better next time." The more regularly you keep this type of journal, the stronger your self-compassion.

42

SELF-DISCLOSURE

· • ● •·

DO YOU EASILY share your experiences and reactions, or do you prefer to keep others at an emotional distance? How difficult is it for you to reveal your joys, goals, and disappointments? It's increasingly clear that your answers bear strongly on happiness. More than fifty years ago, the visionary psychologist Sidney Jourard developed the concept of self-disclosure. During a prolific period that ended with Jourard's sudden, accidental death in 1974, his work on this topic influenced not only American psychology but our broader culture as well. His work shows that the extent to which we're able to reveal ourselves to other people has important consequences for our social relationships—and for our individual well-being as well.

"You cannot love your spouse, your child, or your friend unless he has permitted you to know him and to know what he needs to move forward toward greater health and well-being," Jourard wrote in his ground-breaking article. He followed up with a series of books, including *The Transparent Self*, about self-disclosure in daily life—and, since then, a host of psychological studies have confirmed his viewpoint. Both men and women have greater satisfaction when self-disclosure is present, especially in romantic relationships such as dating and marriage, and it's linked to two aspects: (1) feeling that we can confide easily in our partner and (2) feeling that our partner is emotionally open too. Research consistently shows that spouses tend to match each other in how much they self-reveal, and that cultural forces are potent. For example, Latin Americans self-disclose more than their northerly counterparts—and often view them as emotionally "cold." However, people in both cultures avoid talking about family conflict and sex. Latinos are generally more willing to talk about a wider range of topics— including personal taste in music, movies, and hobbies.

It's also clear that self-disclosure has a beneficial, reciprocal effect; novelist Jane Austen seems to have been mistaken when she wrote that "happiness in marriage is entirely a matter of chance." There's solid evidence that when we hear someone reveal personal information in conversation, we become more forthcoming too. The disclosure leads the other person, in turn, to self-reveal more deeply. A study led by Dr. Sabine Trepte at the University of Hamburg in Germany found this pattern to be true for online communication in social media as well.

Self-disclosure isn't important only in romantic relationships. It also seems vital for emotional intimacy between parents and children. In a recent study that I conducted with colleagues, young adults felt significantly closer to mothers and fathers who reminisced about their childhood, adolescence, and young adulthood compared to those with aloof parents—and were likelier to seek their help or advice. The takeaway is clear: If you'd like your children to be close and value your guidance, then talk freely with them about your life experiences.

Does this mean to reveal everything? Of course not. As Jourard would surely have agreed, it's necessary to use sound judgment in what you disclose to others—whether as parent or spouse, friend or colleague. Especially concerning the workplace, most psychologists recommend caution about what to share. Still, most of us would benefit by unbottling what's inside us.

Letting Down Your Mask

· · · · · · · · · · · · ·

To strengthen your ability to self-disclose to family members or friends, start with small matters—like opening up about recent TV shows, movies, or books that have moved you in some way. But remember: Avoid intellectualization, and keep the focus on your feelings.

43

SENSE of WONDER

• • ● • •

"IMAGINATION IS MORE important than knowledge," Albert Einstein insisted, "for knowledge is limited, whereas imagination embraces the entire world." In his widely read philosophical essays, the Nobel Prize winner extolled wonder as a key driver for both creativity and scientific discovery—and urged that schools better cultivate this trait.

Einstein, of course, was speaking from his vantage point as a physicist, but wonder has long been prized by poets, who have linked it to such qualities as aesthetic delight, surprise, and joyfulness. During the Romantic era of the early nineteenth century, Samuel Coleridge and William Wordsworth deliberately sought to spur a renewed appreciation for the great mystery of life. Wordsworth especially cherished nature as a catalyst for such an awareness, asserting in his famous poem "Lines Written a Few Miles above Tintern Abbey" that, "All which we behold is full of blessings." In his view, daily existence in bustling society inevitably brings boredom and inner weariness. To achieve happiness, it's therefore necessary to see the world afresh. How? By cultivating a sense of wonder, best induced by nature that "never did betray the heart that loved her."

Though for many decades academic psychology had little interest in this trait, the situation abruptly changed with Abraham Maslow's studies of self-actualizing men and women—individuals who maximized their potential in daily life. Maslow found that these highly successful, creative people had frequent peak experiences—whose essence was a sense of wonder. In later writings, Maslow echoed Einstein's call for educators to promote more experiences of wonderment, in order to produce scientists and artists with greater creativity.

In earlier times, organized religion provided a sense of wonder to ordinary as well as highly talented individuals. Sacred texts such as the Bible inspired

the imagination of countless generations via tales of
angels and wise kings, prophetic dreamers and giants,
apocalyptic battles and journeys to heaven. It seems
no historical coincidence that precisely when such
religious narratives lost much of their popular allure
in the Industrial Age, their place was taken by fantasy
and science fiction—offering fresh images and ways
of experiencing the universe. As literary critic David
Hartwell commented in his 1996 book *Age of Wonders*,
"Science fiction has claimed the domains of time
(especially the distant future) and space, the infinite
possibilities out there, just at the moment when the
last locations of awe and mystery have disappeared
from our planet—terra incognito, distant islands, for-
bidden Tibet, the mysterious East."

It's not surprising, then, that one of the few sure
predictors of adult creativity is a youthful interest in
science fiction. Nor is it startling to learn that Maslow
himself—one of America's most creative psychological thinkers—valued this genre as a valuable source
of new ideas about human nature and society. More
recently, Dr. Tonie Stolberg of England's Birmingham

University has studied real experiences of wonderment in the life histories of college students planning a career in science education. More than 90 percent reported at least one experience of wonderment, such as visiting the Grand Canyon or gazing at a beautiful rainbow. Exactly as Einstein would have predicted, such experiences heightened their interest in teaching science.

Fuel Your Imagination

To strengthen your sense of wonder, it's important to nurture your imagination. An excellent way is to keep a dream diary, for dreams alter our perceptions of time and space. Each morning, write down your dream, even if it's only fragmentary. Over time, you'll find that your dream recall improves. Also indulge in science fiction and fantasy to enhance your imaginative faculty. Books are more useful than movies in this regard, as you'll be tapping into your own wellsprings more deeply.

44

TAI CHI

· • ● •·

"THERE ARE TWO kinds of strengths," Shaolin
master Kan told his young disciple in the TV series
Kung Fu. "The outer strength is obvious. It fades with
age. . . . Then there is the *Chi*—the inner strength. It is
more difficult to develop [but] it lasts through every
heat and cold, through old age and beyond." The
series, launched soon after President Richard Nixon's
historic trip to China in 1972, introduced millions of
viewers to ancient Chinese philosophy and martial
arts. For most Westerners at the time, the idea that
an invisible energy permeates all living things—and
that health depends on its balanced flow—seemed
absurd. Today, traditional Chinese medical practices

such as acupuncture are widely accepted among health professionals, and body-energy disciplines for daily well-being—especially Tai Chi—are sprouting as never before.

Historians believe that Tai Chi originated in medieval China as a self-defense practice without weapons. Over the ensuing centuries, a variety of styles developed, as did variations within each style. Though accounts of the history of Tai Chi often differ, the most consistently important—and semi-legendary—figure is a Taoist monk named Chang San-Feng. It's said that he observed five animals—tiger, dragon, leopard, snake, and crane—and decided that the snake and crane, because of their flowing movements, were ablest in overcoming strong, unyielding opponents. Chang replaced brute force with flexibility and suppleness in Chinese martial arts. Historians also link Tai Chi with *qigong*—an ancient discipline with roots in traditional Chinese medicine and Taoism.

Within the Tai Chi system, human beings are posited as miniature versions of the cosmos, and likewise

comprise a constant interplay of five "elements"—
earth, fire, metal, water, and wood. In Chinese medicine, these five elements flow in an interrelated
manner throughout the organs of the body. The formal
name, *t'ai chi ch'uan* ("supreme ultimate fist"), was
coined in the seventeenth century as a new form of
kung fu designed to develop mind-body principles into
both a martial art and exercise for health. In modern
times, Tai Chi evolved into three main forms, named
for their originators: Wu, Yang, and Chen. The slower
Tai Chi movements have most popularly taken root in
the United States, where an estimated 2.3 to 3 million
people practice them regularly—combining gentle
physical exercise and stretching. Each Tai Chi posture
flows into the next without pause, ensuring that one's
body is in constant motion.

Does Tai Chi benefit mind and body? Research
supported by the National Center for Complementary
and Alternative Medicine indicates the practice helps
those with such conditions as osteoarthritis and
symptoms of fibromyalgia, and improves sleep quality

and balance in older adults. A study led by Dr. Leigh Callahan at the University of North Carolina showed that arthritis patients who took an eight-week course improved their physical strength and well-being compared to controls. And Dr. Chenchen Wang's team at Tufts University in Massachusetts found Tai Chi effective in boosting self-esteem, as well as in reducing anxiety, mood disturbance, and stress.

continued ➡

Find Balance

. . . .

Tai Chi is a gentle body-energy system, but it requires mastery. After you find a good class, here are five tips:

1) Choose the best style to achieve your goals. If you're interested in meditation, Wu's the one.

2) Always be aware of your base. It is your link to the ground.

3) Feel the interconnectedness of your whole body. Physical movements are less important than your overall body harmony.

4) Be patient with your progress. Teachers say that Chi can't be rushed.

5) To enhance your motivation and fun, practice with a friend in a park or garden.

45

TEARS of JOY

· · • · ·

HAVE YOU EVER cried from happiness? Do you become dewy-eyed from inspiring music, art, or literature—or from the victory of your favorite sports team? Can you recall movies whose uplifting scenes moved you to tears? Ancient literary sources such as the Bible and the Greek *Iliad* show clearly that people for millennia have cried in happiness. But when and why? And are such tears healthy for us? Literary giants have long expressed their viewpoints.

The English Romantic poet William Wordsworth saw nature as a main catalyst for this phenomenon—and extolled the power of magnificent landscapes to exalt us. Yet, in an intriguing 1850 essay called *The Poetic Principle*, Edgar Allan Poe argued instead that aesthetics—especially music—has the greatest power to make people cry. In his view, we cry from experiences of beauty because they remind us of our separation from the divine.

When psychology became established as a science, its founders gave little attention to positive emotions. Behaviorist leaders like B. F. Skinner ignored the entire emotional realm for its inherently subjective nature. And when post–World War II psychoanalysts analyzed the phenomenon of crying from happiness, they followed Sigmund Freud's cynicism by declaring that tears of seeming joy are actually tears of sadness. That is, parents cry at their daughter's wedding not from happiness for her romantic bliss, but from having lost their "little girl" forever. In the psychoanalytic view, nobody ever really cries in joy, but only with masked emotional pain.

But times change, and the role of positive emotions is now proving crucial for our well-being. There's mounting scientific evidence that it's not enough just to avoid habitually feeling lonely, worried, or depressed. If you really want to flourish, you've got to connect meaningfully with your environment, especially with other people. In this new light, tears of joy—involving both intense and positive feelings—make up a fascinating area of study. Since 2013, I've led an international team to better understand the causes and benefits of tears of joy.

What have we found? Because the experience of joyful tears has never been mapped before, our initial goal was to determine what types of situations cause people to cry in happiness. We were surprised when eighteen different categories emerged—including some we'd never anticipated. Several of the categories involved familial affection, such as attending a wedding or graduation ceremony, the birth of a child, romantic ardor, attainment of a personal goal, or a reunion. In results that should warm the hearts of media moguls, many people also reported crying joyfully from an inspiring movie, TV program, or book. Some even mentioned the same movie—Frank Capra's 1946 classic *It's a Wonderful Life.*

We also found that tears of joy aren't rare, though national differences do exist. For instance, more than

30 percent of Americans and Venezuelans reported that they had cried from happiness in the previous month, and so did nearly 10 percent of over 250 Japanese college students. Generally, people reported feeling better physically and often had lowered mental stress, as well, after experiencing tears of joy. Intriguingly, we also found that people who had more recently cried in happiness had the highest self-reported level of health.

Let Happiness Flow

. . . .

Though it's difficult to induce such intense outpourings, you can probably increase their likelihood by recalling when you last cried in joy. What triggered it for you? Were you alone or with others? And, how did your body feel as tears came forth? Your answers will best guide you to evoke such experiences in the future.

46

TIME AFFLUENCE

· · ● ··

"WE ALL HAVE all the time there is," declared Eleanor Roosevelt, America's most popular first lady, in *You Learn by Living*. "No one can tell you how to use your time. It is yours." Published in 1960, her book of advice for youth marked an era when two-hour work-day lunches were common—and futurists worried about how most Americans would use their enormous, anticipated leisure in coming decades. Thanks to increasing automation, most social scientists were sure that employment pressures and household drudgery would greatly diminish—allowing virtually everyone a feast of recreational opportunities.

Fast-forward to today—and this prediction seems laughable. Although belief in a society with huge leisure just around the corner remained dominant for another few decades, experts eventually changed their view. As early as 1980, Dr. David Elkind warned in *The Hurried Child* that children were now subjected to unprecedented rushing in their everyday lives. A decade later, the future was looking so different that books with titles like Juliet Schor's *The Overworked American* were common, but empirical data remained sparse.

Among the first social scientists to measure the problem was Dr. Leslie Perlow at Harvard University—and her descriptor *time famine* quickly caught on among social scientists. Studying a team of software engineers who constantly felt they had too much to do and not enough time do it, Perlow concluded that corporations were actually crippling their workers' productivity by placing them in "fast-paced, high-pressure, and crisis-filled" settings. More recently, psychologists Drs. Tim Kasser and Kennon Sheldon developed the concept of *time affluence*—the sense that one regularly has plentiful time at hand. Across four studies, they found that—even after controlling for material wealth—individual experience of time affluence was linked to greater happiness. Intriguingly, too, those who reported close relationships generally had more time affluence than others. The researchers concluded that feelings of time affluence not only benefited people's physical health and social involvements, but also their inner well-being.

Expanding upon such work, Dr. Cassie Mogilner of the Wharton School of Business and her colleagues experimentally found that, in a seeming paradox, our sense of time affluence *increases* when we spend time helping others. How is this possible? In their view, it's because such altruistic behavior boosts our self-esteem and self-confidence—and thereby stretches our time in our minds. Ultimately, we become more likely to commit to future engagements, despite our busy schedules. A follow-up article in the *Harvard Business Review* headlined: "You'll Feel Less Rushed if You Give Time Away."

How do experts themselves strive for time affluence? Kasser, a married father with two teenagers, commented, "Almost every year, I've consistently made arrangements with my college to work either two-thirds or three-quarters time, and get paid accordingly. For twelve years, my wife worked half time, for no more than thirty weeks a year. We made these decisions so that we had more time for our sons, our community involvement, each other, and ourselves."

Give Hours to Get Hours

. . . .

To enhance your sense of time affluence and resulting productivity, become more generous with the hours at your weekly disposal. Build into your routine helping activities to benefit others, whether family members, friends, or those in your larger community. Saunter and stroll rather than hurry. As J. R .R. Tolkien advised, "Not all those who wander are lost." Remember, the less you hoard your time, the more plentiful it will appear in your daily life.

47

tRAVEl

· • ● • ·

DO YOU LIKE to travel? For many people, it's one of life's most fulfilling experiences—not only inducing happy relaxation, but also offering new philosophical and spiritual horizons. Precisely from this latter viewpoint, Mark Twain (Samuel Clemens) declared that, "Travel is fatal to prejudice, bigotry, and narrow-mindedness. Broad, wholesome, charitable views of [people] and things cannot be acquired by vegetating in one little corner of the earth all one's lifetime."

Though Twain was no psychologist, this sentiment from *The Innocents Abroad*, his first, and most popular book in his lifetime—published in 1869—has strong support from those today advocating travel for personal growth. By chronicling a true-life, grueling excursion from New York City to Europe and the Holy Land, Twain in midlife had already reaped considerable benefit by traveling far beyond the confines of his boyhood hometown of Hannibal, Missouri. He would eventually become an international celebrity for his entertaining public readings.

Such founders of modern psychology as Alfred Adler and Carl Jung traveled extensively and joyfully to promote their work. Both not only reveled in the attention they received from diverse audiences, but also gained important insights into how cultures influence personality. Sigmund Freud achieved an international breakthrough in voyaging to the United States to present his ideas to American colleagues, and always enjoyed foreign sightseeing. Yet, surprisingly, none of these men ever discussed the psychological benefits of travel.

Fortunately, this situation is now changing. Among the world's leading researchers in this area is Dr. Sebastian Filep of the University of Otago in New Zealand. In recent years, his studies have highlighted the link between tourist experiences and positive functioning—especially that of *flow* (see *Flow*, page 78). Flow during travel may arise, for example, when we're captivated by beautiful scenery or historic architecture—and fall into a dreamy, delicious sense of timelessness. Freud powerfully experienced this phenomenon in his first visit to Rome.

In forging a new approach to tourism, Dr. Filep identifies five different types of experience, each with its particular value: (1) *recreational*, which provides general well-being and idle pleasure; (2) *diversionary*, which mainly offers distraction from current stress; (3) *experiential*, involving a search for self-authenticity; (4) *experimental*, which involves a search for alternative ways of living; and (5) *existential*, which may transform our habitual patterns of thinking or acting. Though we're perhaps most likely to gain flow via the fun of *recreational* and *diversionary* tourism, it's probably the *existential* mode that leads most to enduring change within.

There's also evidence that foreign travel enhances our creativity. In research that has generated substantial interest in the business community, Dr. Adam

Galinsky at Northwestern University and his colleagues found that MBA students, both in the United States and Europe, who had lived abroad were significantly more creative on a variety of problem-solving tasks. In the researchers' view, the experience of living abroad enhances receptivity to new meanings for everyday situations. Such travel also seems to increase our readiness to accept ideas from unfamiliar sources—thereby facilitating the unconscious, creative process. New findings generated by Lile Jia at the University of Indiana suggest that simply placing ourselves in a "traveling mindset" may also improve creative problem solving.

Meaningful Journeys

· · · · · · · · · · · ·

It's not always possible to travel whenever we want, but we can always reflect on what we've experienced. Take a few minutes to answer these questions: How has travel strengthened your open-mindedness, and your appreciation of beauty and excellence? How about your gratitude? In what ways do you think that travel enhances your own creativity and problem-solving ability? Where would you most like to travel next, and why?

48

VOLUNtEERING

· • ● •·

"ASK NOT WHAT your country can do for you. Ask what you can do for your country," urged John F. Kennedy in his inaugural address. On that frosty day in January 1961, he stood on the newly renovated East Front of the U.S. Capitol and appealed to idealism— among Americans and "fellow citizens of the world." Five weeks later, Kennedy's executive order established the nation's Peace Corps, signifying official support for American volunteerism in economically developing nations. Though some subsequent public service programs have come and gone, and the Peace Corps itself has never had strong congressional support, volunteerism has become a major psychological focus.

In fields ranging from secondary education to gerontology, researchers are increasingly confirming the impact of service on individual well-being. As early as adolescence, the impact is substantial, and it exists all the way into old age. Under the banner of *positive youth development* (as professionals call it), studies show that teens who volunteer are less likely to become pregnant or use drugs—and are more likely to have positive academic, psychological, and occupational well-being—than non-volunteering peers.

There's an important health payoff as well. As reported by Dr. Hannah Schreier at New York's Mount Sinai School of Medicine and her colleagues, tenth-graders who participated in a two-month mentoring program with elementary-school-age children showed lower cholesterol levels and body mass compared to controls. Intriguingly, the effect was greatest for teens who became more empathic and altruistic by volunteering. Dr. Jane Pilavin at the University of Wisconsin found that even at-risk adolescents who volunteer reap benefits in greater self-esteem, social connection, and sense of belongingness. In Pilavin's view, such traits helped teens resist the emotionally harmful effects of bullying.

How about for midlife and beyond? In a study by Drs. Peggy Thoits and Lyndi Hewitt at Vanderbilt University, volunteering adults scored higher than non-volunteers on six aspects of personal well-being: (1) happiness, (2) life satisfaction, (3) self-esteem, (4) sense of control over life, (5) physical health, and (6) infrequency of depression. The researchers also found evidence for a personality-and-volunteerism "cycle" in which people who are happier, and have higher self-esteem and less depression, are more likely to volunteer—thereby even further boosting their well-being. More recently, Drs. Martin Binder and Andreas Freytag reported in the *Journal of Economic Psychology* that volunteerism sustained over time steadily raised individuals' happiness, and, strikingly, no "drop-off effect" in mood occurred. The investigators argued that public policy-makers should more strongly encourage adult volunteering—for example, by publicizing its payoff in greater personal happiness.

For those in their retirement years, the scientific evidence is likewise strong. In a representative study, Dr. Nancy Morrow-Howell of Washington University and her colleagues found that older adults who volunteer—and who engage in more hours of volunteering—report higher levels of well-being, regardless of gender or race, compared to non-volunteers similar in mental and physical health.

continued ➡

Do Good, Then Feel Great

With countless opportunities available for volunteering, what's best for you? Here are five tips:

1) Know the causes that personally interest you—whether improving parks, joining the arts council, or reading to schoolchildren.

2) Identify the skills you can offer.

3) Decide whether you want to learn something new. Many organizations will train volunteers.

4) Don't overcommit. Balance your time carefully to avoid extra stress or burnout.

5) Consider volunteering with family members or friends. You're likely to become closer by serving others.

49

WISDOM

· · ● ··

"GET WISDOM, AND whatever you get, get insight."
So counsels the biblical Book of Proverbs, traditionally attributed to King Solomon. Such advice is surely
relevant in the twenty-first century, but what exactly
is wisdom and what is insight? Does wisdom make
us happier—as the Roman emperor and philosopher
Marcus Aurelius insisted? How can we measure and
foster it? Positive psychologists today are increasingly
grappling with these challenging questions. And a
new therapeutic specialty, known as *philosophical
counseling*, has simultaneously arisen.

Of course, the idea that philosophy has healing
power when it involves guided questioning dates
far back—to the Socrates of Plato's dialogues some

2,400 years ago. In Plato's *Apology*, his teacher Socrates defends himself against charges of corrupting the young men of Athens by arguing that his constant questioning was aimed only at helping them to care "for the best possible state of [their] souls." In medieval times, the rabbinic physician Maimonides likewise linked well-being with philosophical rigor—and gave practical advice on how to become a sage by strengthening mind and body.

With the rise of modern psychology in the early twentieth century, wisdom fell on hard times, as it had traditionally been associated with religion, not science. Freud's notion of unconscious motivation also made it seem like a naughty clown lurked inside us all. Until recently, too, wisdom seemed too subjective for rigorous study. After all, other than Yoda in *Star Wars*—or wizardly Gandalf in Tolkien's *Lord of the Rings*—could anyone be universally acknowledged to possess this quality?

Over the past twenty years, though, two scientific perspectives have emerged. The first, associated with the Max Planck Institute for Human Development in

Berlin, views wisdom as a type of outstanding "expertise" in dealing with life's meaning and conduct. For these researchers, it comprises "knowledge with extraordinary scope, depth, measure, and balance"—and can best be determined by convening panels of scholars in fields like philosophy. In contrast, Dr. Monika Ardelt at the University of Florida at Gainesville and her adherents see wisdom as embedded within ordinary people's decisions in daily life—not as abstract principles to be uncovered by academicians—and rooted in empathy. Neither approach views wisdom as synonymous with intelligence; both regard learning from life experience as crucial.

However wisdom is defined, does it really help us to flourish? A study by Dr. Ardelt showed that wisdom is significantly linked to life satisfaction for both men and women—strikingly, even a better predictor than objective circumstances such as physical health. Researchers at the Max Planck Institute found that wise people value personal growth, insight, and friendship more than creature comfort. They also prefer resolving conflicts via win-win solutions, rather than situations where one gains at another's expense. More recently, Dr. Igor Grossman at the University of Waterloo in Ontario, Canada, and his colleagues found that wiser people have higher life satisfaction, better social relations, less brooding—and greater longevity than their less-wise peers.

Concurrent with such research has been the growth of *philosophical counseling*—a new field in which academically trained philosophers guide people seeking meaning, purpose, or fulfillment. More like highly intellectual life coaches than traditional therapists, they offer wisdom from the ages to help solve personal dilemmas—on topics such as coping with an ethical crisis at work or overcoming boredom.

If the idea of philosophical counseling appeals to you, reading Lao Tzu or Albert Camus might be your cup of tea.

Learn from a Wise Mind

· · · · · · · · · · · · · ·

Interview someone whom you consider wise, perhaps a family member, friend, or clergy.

Your questions might include:

* In your view, what exactly is wisdom?

* Do people usually become wiser with age? If so, how?

* Is wisdom the same thing as intelligence or knowledge?

* What advice would you give to a younger person who wants to gain more wisdom?

50

ZEN MEDITATION

· · • · ·

WHAT COMES TO mind when you hear the word *meditation*? Not long ago, it seems, the practice was mainly associated with skinny Hindu ascetics wearing loincloths and turbans. The term itself usually connoted the arcane dogmas of a vanished time, and the claims made by supporters seemed almost impossible. How could people learn to control their heartbeat or respiration simply by staring at their navel or at a colorful symbol? The idea that we might be able to regulate our autonomic nervous system or direct our fleeting thoughts appeared nonsensical. Outside of a few zealous devotees, there was meager interest in meditation.

How the situation has changed! Not only is this ancient practice taught in countless yoga centers throughout the United States and abroad, but it's become well accepted in health-care training as well. Typically, meditative practices associated with Buddhism, Christianity, Hinduism, Judaism, Sufism, and other spiritual traditions are taught as distinct from rituals and beliefs. In this way, major medical journals such as *Digestion*, *Hypertension*, *Pain Medicine*, and *Sleep* all regularly publish articles on meditation's effectiveness for a variety of ailments. These include anxiety, asthma, chronic pain, digestive disorders, hypertension, insomnia, and various forms of addiction. Meanwhile, neuroscience researchers are seeking to unravel precisely how meditation actually works.

Among this movement's leaders is Dr. James Austin, a neurology professor at the University of Missouri at Columbia. Since his first trip to Japan in 1974 to learn Zen Buddhist meditation, he has been investigating three key mysteries: How does the human brain actually function? What really occurs during extraordinary mental states such as enlightenment? What role does meditation play in leading to higher states of awareness?

Stimulated by these questions, Austin has written lucidly on Zen mysticism from the standpoint of neuroscience theory and research. In his view, the actual experience of enlightenment—which depends on sustained meditative practice—comprises two aspects: (1) a loss of the sense of "self" basic to ordinary consciousness and (2) a corresponding feeling of oneness with the entire world.

After a mystical experience at a London subway station, Austin became convinced that our brain is "hardwired" for such events and that meditation effectively releases preexisting neurological functions. He also reported that his mystical experience produced immediate and enduring inner benefits—such as greater calmness and equanimity.

While many types of mediation have flourished historically, most share these four features:

1. the choice of a quiet location with as few distractions as possible

2. a comfortable posture (whether sitting, lying down, or walking)

3. focusing one's attention through a specially chosen word or phrase, image, or sensation of the breath

4. having an open or receptive attitude, in which one lets go of passing thoughts without judgment or suppression

Best results are usually obtained by practicing one particular technique rather than a variety. As the Vietnamese Buddhist monk Thich Nhat Hanh has observed, "Meditation can help us embrace our worries, fear, our anger—and that is very healing."

Refresh with a Breath

Set a timer for fifteen minutes, sit in a comfortable position, and close your eyes. Focus your attention on your breath as it departs, then returns to your nostrils. Don't alter your breathing pattern. Just be aware of your breath and how it flows evenly through you. As you inhale, feel the energy that you're absorbing from the air fill your being with vitality. Exhale, feeling all tension dissipate from your body—leaving you refreshed. When the timer goes off, slowly rise and continue your day.

··•   REFERENCES   •··

INTRODUCTION

Freud, Sigmund. *Wit and Its Relation to the Unconscious.* Translated by A.
A. Brill. New York: Dover, 2011.

The English Standard Bible with Apocrypha, Book of Psalms, 118:24.
New York: Oxford University Press, 2009.

Ibid. Book of Proverbs, 17:22.

James, William. *Principles of Psychology, Volume 1.* Cambridge: Harvard
University Press, 1981.

1 ACTING IMPROV

Abele, Robert. "Alan Arkin, Totally in CONTROL." *Los Angeles Times,* June
19, 2008. Accessed July 18, 2015. http://articles.latimes.com/2008/
jun/19/entertainment/et-arkin19.

Alter, Alexandra. "Two Protons Walk into a Black Hole, and Other Jokes
Physicists Tell." *Wall Street Journal,* September 4, 2008. Accessed July
18, 2015. http://www.wsj.com/articles/SB122048206487796841.

Chandler, Barb. "Parallels between Improv Comedy and Therapy." *Psych
Central,* January 30, 2013. Accessed July 27, 2015. http://psychcentral.
com/lib/parallels-between-improv-comedy-and-therapy/.

"Improv Your Counseling." The website of University of the Rockies.
Accessed July 12, 2015. http://www.rockies.edu/news/
detail.php?id=406.

Kelly, Kip. "Leadership Agility: Using Improv to Build Critical Skills."
Presentation, UNC Kenan-Flagler Business School, 2012.

Louden, Kathleen. "Improv for Anxiety: A Stand-Up Therapeutic Tool?"
Medscape, April 14, 2014. Accessed July 18, 2015. http://www
.medscape.com/viewarticle/823580.

2 ADVENTURE SPORTS

Garfield, Charles A., and Hal Z. Bennett. *Peak Performance: Mental
Training Techniques of the World's Greatest Athletes.* New York:
Warner, 1985.

Humberstone, Barbara. "Adventurous Activities, Embodiment
and Nature: Spiritual, Sensual, and Sustainable? Embodying
Environmental Justice." *Motriz: Revista de Educação Física* 19, no. 3
(2013): 565–571.

Jackson, Susan A., Patrick R. Thomas, Herbert W. Marsh, and Christopher J. Smethurst. "Relationships between Flow, Self-Concept, Psychological Skills, and Performance." *Journal of Applied Sport Psychology* 13, no. 2 (2001): 129–153.

Kerr, John H., and Susan Houge Mackenzie. "Multiple Motives for Participating in Adventure Sports." *Psychology of Sport and Exercise* 13, no. 5 (2012): 649–657.

Murphy, Michael, and Rhea White. *In the Zone: Transcendent Experience in Sports.* New York: Penguin, 1995.

Sheard, Michael, and Jim Golby. "The Efficiency of an Outdoor Adventure Education Curriculum on Selected Aspects of Positive Psychological Development." *Journal of Experiential Education* 29, no. 2 (2006): 187–209.

3 ART APPRECIATION

Cuypers, Koenraad, et al. "Patterns of Receptive and Creative Cultural Activities and Their Association with Perceived Health, Anxiety, Depression and Satisfaction with Life among Adults: The HUNT Study, Norway." *Journal of Epidemiology and Community Health* 66, no. 8 (2012): 698–703.

Fujiwara, Daniel. "Museums and Happiness: The Value of Participating in Museums and the Arts." Presentation, Museum of East Anglian Life, April 2013.

Lieberman, E. James. *Acts of Will: The Life and Work of Otto Rank.* New York: Free Press, 1998.

Packer, Jan. "Visitors' Restorative Experiences in Museum and Botanic Garden Environments." In *Tourist Experience and Fulfillment: Insights from Positive Psychology*, edited by S. Filep and P. Pearce. New York: Routledge, 2014, 202–222.

Rank, Otto. *Art and Artist.* New York: Norton, 1989.

Rosenbloom, Stephanie. "The Art of Slowing Down in a Museum." *New York Times*, October 9, 2014. Accessed July 12, 2015. http://nyti.ms/1xu0de8.

Wilkinson, Rebecca A., and Gioia Chilton. "Positive Art Therapy: Linking Positive Psychology to Art Therapy Theory, Practice, and Research." *Art Therapy* 30, no. 1 (2013): 4–11.

4 AUTHENTICITY

Kernis, Michael H., and Brian M. Goldman. "From Thought and Experience to Behavior and Interpersonal Relationships: A Multicomponent Conceptualization of Authenticity." In *On Building, Defending, and Regulating the Self: A Psychological Perspective*, edited by A. Tesser, J. Wood, and D. Stapel. New York: Psychology Press, 2005, 31–52.

Kirschenbaum, Howard. *The Life and Work of Carl Rogers*. Washington, D.C: American Counseling Association, 2008.

Moustakas, Clark. *The Self: Explorations in Personal Growth*. New York: Colophon, 1975.

Rogers, Carl. *On Becoming a Person*. Boston: Houghton Mifflin, 1961.

Shakespeare, William. *Hamlet*. New York: Simon & Schuster, 1992.

Warner, C. Terry, and Terrance D. Olson. "Another View of Family Conflict and Family Wholeness." *Family Relations* 30, no. 4 (1981): 492–503.

Wood, Alex M., et al. "The Authentic Personality: A Theoretical and Empirical Conceptualization and the Development of the Authenticity Scale." *Journal of Counseling Psychology* 55, no. 3 (2008): 385–399.

5 AWE

Heschel, Abraham Joshua. *God in Search of Man*. New York: Farrar, Straus & Giroux, 1976.

Hoffman, Edward. *The Right to be Human: A Biography of Abraham Maslow*, 2nd edition. New York: McGraw-Hill, 1999.

James, William. *The Varieties of Religious Experience*. New York: Penguin, 1982.

Keltner, Dacher, and Jonathon Haidt. "Approaching Awe, a Moral, Spiritual, and Aesthetic Emotion." *Cognition and Emotion* 17, no. 2 (2003): 297–314.

Schneider, Kirk. *Awakening to Awe*. New York: Aronson, 2009.

———. "Awe-Based Learning." *Shift: At the Frontiers of Consciousness* 8 (2005): 16–19.

6 BIRDING

Bailey, Florence Merriam. *Birds Through an Opera Glass*. New York: Chautauqua Press, 1889.

Berger, Michele. "New USFWS Report: 46.7 Million People Call Themselves Bird Watchers." Audubon, August 23, 2012. Accessed July 15, 2015. http://www.audubon.org/news/ new-usfws-report-467-million-people-call-themselves-birdwatchers.

Dickinson, Emily. *A Spicing of Birds*. Middletown, Conn.: Wesleyan University Press, 2004.

Dunlap, Thomas R. *In the Field, Among the Feathered: A History of Birders and Their Guides*. Oxford, UK: Oxford University Press, 2014.

Ratcliffe, Eleanor, Birgitta Gatersleben, and Paul T. Sowden. "Bird Sounds and Their Contributions to Perceived Attention Restoration and Stress Recovery." *Journal of Environmental Psychology* 36 (2013): 221–228.

7 COMMUNITY SINGING

Bailey, Betty A., and Jane W. Davidson. "Effects of Group Singing and Performance for Marginalized and Middle-Class Singers." *Psychology of Music* 33, no. 3 (2005): 269–303.

Clift, Stephen, and Grenville Hancox. "The Significance of Choral Singing for Sustaining Psychological Well-Being: Findings from a Survey of Choristers in England, Australia, and Germany." *Music Performance Research* 3, no. 1 (2010): 79–96.

Hoffman, Edward. *The Drive for Self: Alfred Adler and the Founding of Individual Psychology*. Reading, Mass.: Addison-Wesley, 1994.

Liebert, Georges, and David Pellauer. *Nietzsche and Music*. Chicago: University of Chicago, 2004.

Watanabe, Hideo. "Changing Adult Learning in Japan: The Shift from Traditional Singing to Karaoke." *International Journal of Lifelong Education* 24, no. 3 (2005): 257–267.

8 COOKING AND BAKING

Csikszentmihalyi, Mihaly. *Finding Flow: The Psychology of Engagement with Everyday Life*. New York: Basic Books, 1997.

Csikszentmihalyi, Mihaly, and Judith LeFevre. "Optimal Experience in Work and Leisure." *Journal of Personality and Social Psychology* 56, no. 5 (1989): 815.

Essig, Todd. "Culinary Mindfulness: Something You Won't Hear About at TEDxManhattan." *Forbes*, February 2, 2013. Accessed July 16, 2015. http://www.forbes.com/sites/toddessig/2013/02/14/culinary-mindfulness-something-you-wont-hear-about-at-tedxmanhattan/.

Haley, Lesley, and Elizabeth Anne McKay. "'Baking Gives You Confidence': Users' Views of Engaging in the Occupation of Baking." *British Journal of Occupational Therapy* 67, no. 3 (2004): 125–128.

O'Neill, Molly. "The Zen of Cooking, or Joy When Time Allows." *New York Times*, October 27, 1993. Accessed July 16, 2015. http://www.nytimes.com/1993/10/27/garden/the-zen-of-cooking-or-joy-when-time-allows.html/.

Sager, Mike. "Julia Child: What I've Learned." *Esquire*, August 15, 2015. Accessed July 16, 2015. http://www.esquire.com/food-drink/interviews/a1273/julia-child-quotes-0601/.

9 CREATIVITY

Guilford, J. P. "Creativity." *American Psychologist* 5 (1950): 444–454.

———. *The Nature of Human Intelligence*. New York: McGraw-Hill, 1967.

Scott, Ginamarie, Lyle E. Leritz, and Michael D. Mumford. "The Effectiveness of Creativity Training: A Quantitative Review." *Creativity Research Journal* 16, no. 4 (2004): 361–388.

Simonton, Dean King. "Creativity." In *Handbook of Positive Psychology*, edited by C. R. Snyder and S. J. Lopez. New York: Oxford University Press, 2002, 189–201.

Wilson, Timothy D., et al. "Just Think: The Challenges of the Disengaged Mind." *Science* 345, no. 6192 (2014): 75–77.

Wolf, Gary. "Steve Jobs: The Next Insanely Great Thing." *Wired*, February 1996, http://archive.wired.com/wired/archive/4.02/jobs_pr.html.

10 CURIOSITY

Gruber, Matthias J., Bernard D. Gelman, and Charan Ranganath. "States of Curiosity Modulate Hippocampus-Dependent Learning via the Dopaminergic Circuit." *Neuron* 84, no. 2 (2014): 486–496.

Hoffman, Edward. *The Book of Graduation Wisdom*. Secaucus, N.J.: Citadel, 2003.

Kashdan, Todd B., et al. "Curiosity Protects against Interpersonal Aggression: Cross-Sectional, Daily Process, and Behavioral Evidence." *Journal of Personality* 81, no. 1 (2013): 87–102.

Kashdan, Todd B., Paul Rose, and Frank D. Fincham. "Curiosity and Exploration: Facilitating Positive Subjective Experiences and Personal Growth and Opportunities." *Journal of Personality* 82, no. 3 (2004): 291–305.

Keren, Robert. "Nobel Prize Winning Biologist Says Curiosity Drives Scientific Discovery." *Middlebury*, March 11, 2015. Last accessed July 27, 2015. http://www.middlebury.edu/newsroom/node/492464.

Wilson, Timothy D., et al. "Just Think: The Challenges of the Disengaged Mind." *Science* 345, no. 6192 (2014): 75–77.

11 DANCING

"About Dance/Movement Therapy." The website of the ADTA. Accessed July 12, 2015. http://www.adta.org/About_DMT/.

"About the American Dance Therapy Association." The website of the ADTA. Accessed July 12, 2015. http://www.adta.org/about_adta/.

Devereaux, Christina. "Dance/Movement Therapy and Autism." *Psychology Today*, April 2, 2014. Accessed July 27, 2015. https://www.psychologytoday.com/blog/meaning-in-motion/201404/dancemovement-therapy-and-autism.

Hoffman, Edward. *The Drive for Self: Alfred Adler and the Founding of Individual Psychology.* Reading, Mass.: Addison-Wesley, 1994.

Murcia, Cynthia Quiroga, Stephan Bongard, and Gunter Kreutz. "Emotional and Neurohumoral Responses to Dancing Tango Argentino: The Effects of Music and Partner." *Music and Medicine* 1, no. 1 (2009): 14–21.

Murcia, Cynthia Quiroga, et al. "Shall We Dance? An Exploration of the Perceived Benefits of Dancing on Well-Being." *Arts & Health* 2, no. 2 (2010): 149–163.

Pinniger, Rosa, et al. "Argentine Tango Dance Compared to Mindfulness Meditation and a Waiting-List Control: A Randomised Trial for Treating Depression." *Complementary Therapies in Medicine* 20, no. 6 (2012): 377–384.

12 DOING ART

Friedman, Lawrence J. *Identity's Architect: A Biography of Erik H. Erikson.* New York: Scribner, 1999.

Jung, Carl. *The Red Book.* New York: W. W. Norton, 2009.

May, Rollo. *Existential Psychology.* New York: Crown Publishing Group/Random House, 1969.

———. *The Courage to Create.* London: Collins, 1975.

———. *The Meaning of Anxiety.* 1950. New York: W. W. Norton, 1977.

———. *My Quest for Beauty.* San Francisco: Saybrook, 1985.

Muntz, Eugene. *Michelangelo.* New York: Parkstone Press International, 2005.

13 DREAMS

Freud, Sigmund. *The Interpretation of Dreams.* Translated by James Strachey. New York: Basic Books, 1955.

Hoffman, Edward. *The Way of Splendor: Jewish Mysticism and Modern Psychology.* Lantham, Md.: Rowman & Littlefield, 2006.

———. *The Kabbalah Reader: A Sourcebook of Visionary Judaism.* Boston: Shambhala, 2010.

14 EMPATHY

Adler, Alfred. *The Pattern of Life*, edited by W. B. Wolfe. New York: Greenberg, 1930.

Alper, Robert. *Thanks, I Needed That.* Canton, Mich.: David Crumm Media, 2013.

Dawkins, Richard. *The Selfish Gene.* New York: Oxford University Press, 1990.

Rogers, Carl. "Experiences in Communication." *Listening Way.* Accessed July 21, 2015. http://www.listeningway.com/rogers2-eng.html.

Stern, Jessica A., Jessica L. Borelli, and Patricia A. Smiley. "Assessing Parental Empathy: A Role for Empathy in Child Attachment." *Attachment & Human Development* 17, no. 1 (2015): 1–22.

15 EXPLANATORY STYLE

Emerson, Ralph Waldo. "An Oration Delivered before the Literary Societies of Dartmouth College." Oration at the Literary Societies at Dartmouth College, N.H., July 24, 1838.

Hoffman, Malvina. *Heads and Tales.* Auguste Rodin quote. New York: Bonanza Books, 1936.

Peterson, Christopher, Martin E. P. Seligman, and George E. Vaillant. "Pessimistic Explanatory Style Is a Risk Factor for Physical Illness: A Thirty-Five-Year Longitudinal Study." *Journal of Personality and Social Psychology* 55, no. 1 (1988): 23.

Seligman, Martin E. P. *Learned Optimism*, 2nd ed. New York: Pocket Books, 1998.

———. *Authentic Happiness.* New York: Free Press, 2002.

———. *Flourish: A Visionary New Understanding of Happiness and Well-Being.* New York: Free Press, 2011.

16 EXPRESSIVE WRITING

Lyubomirsky, Sonja, Kennon M. Sheldon, and David Schkade. "Pursuing Happiness: The Architecture of Sustainable Change." *Review of General Psychology* 9, no. 2 (2005): 111.

———. "Putting Stress into Words: Health, Linguistic, and Therapeutic Implications." *Behavior Research and Therapy* 31 (1993): 539–548.

Pennebaker, James W. *Opening Up: The Healing Power of Expressing Emotions*, rev. ed. New York: Guilford Press, 1997.

Pennebaker, James W., and Janel D. Seagal. "Forming a Story: The Health Benefits of Narrative." *Journal of Clinical Psychology* 55 (1999): 1243–1254.

Progoff, Ida. *At a Journal Workshop*, rev. ed. Los Angeles: J. P. Tarcher, 1992.

———. *Life-Study: Experiencing Creative Lives by the Intensive Journal Method*. New York: Dialogue House, 1983.

Wilde, Oscar. *The Importance of Being Earnest*. Mineola, N.Y.: Dover Publications, 1990.

Woolf, Virginia. *A Writer's Diary*. Boston: Mariner Books, 2003.

17 FLOW

Csikszentmihalyi, Mihaly. *Flow: The Psychology of Optimal Experience*. New York: Harper Perennial Modern Classics, 2008.

———. *The Pursuit of Happiness*. Accessed July 21, 2015. http://www.pursuit-of-happiness.org/history-of-happiness/mihaly-csikszentmihalyi/.

Klee, Paul, and Felix Klee. *The Diaries of Paul Klee, 1898–1918*. Berkeley: University of California Press, 1964.

Robinson, Jon. "Kobe Bryant Interview." *IGN*, August 21, 2006, http://www.ign.com/articles/2006/08/21/kobe-bryant-interview.

18 FORGIVENESS

Enright, Robert D. *Forgiveness Is a Choice: A Step-by-Step Process for Resolving Anger and Restoring Hope*. Washington, D.C.: American Psychological Association, 2001.

Friedberg, Jennifer P., Sonia Suchday, and V. S. Srinivas. "Relationship Between Forgiveness and Psychological and Physiological Indices in Cardiac Patients." *International Journal of Behavioral Medicine* 16, no. 3 (2009): 205–211.

Gandhi, Mahatma. "Interview to the Press." *Young India*. April 2, 1931.

King, Coretta Scott, and Martin Luther King III. *The Words of Martin Luther King, Jr.: Second Edition*. New York: William Morrow Paperbacks, 2001.

Lawler, Kathleen A., et al. "The Unique Effects of Forgiveness on Health: An Exploration of Pathways." *Journal of Behavioral Medicine* 28, no. 2 (2005): 157–167.

Matan, Kazimierz. "Who Was Paul Boese?" *Answers.com*. Accessed July 27, 2015. http://www.answers.com/Q/Who_was_Paul_Boese.

19 FRIENDSHIP

Adler, Alfred. *Social Interest: A Challenge to Mankind*. New York: Greenberg, 1938.

Aristotle. *The Works of Aristotle, Vol. 9, Nicomachean Ethics*, edited by W. D. Ross. Oxford, UK: Clarendon Press, 1908.

Hoffman, Edward. *The Wisdom of Maimonides: The Life and Writings of the Jewish Sage*. Boston: Shambhala/Trumpeter, 2009.

Surtees, Paul G., Nicholas W. J. Wainwright, and Kay-Tee Khaw. "Obesity, Confidant Support, and Functional Health: Cross-Sectional Evidence from the EPIC-Norfolk Cohort." *International Journal of Obesity and Related Metabolic Disorders* 28 (2004): 748–758.

20 GARDENING

Austen, Jane. *Jane Austen's Letters*, edited by Deirdre Le Faye. New York: Oxford University Press, 2014.

Ginzberg, Louis. *Legends of the Bible*. Philadelphia: Jewish Publication Society of America, 1975.

Hazen, Teresia. "Therapeutic Garden Characteristics." *American Horticultural Therapy Association* 41, no. 2 (2012).

Hoffman, Edward. *The Right to Be Human: A Biography of Abraham Maslow*, 2nd ed. New York: McGraw-Hill, 1999.

Hoffman, Edward, and David Castro-Blanco. "Horticultural Therapy with a Four-Year-Old Boy: A Case Report." *Journal of Therapeutic Horticulture* 10 (1988): 3–8.

Seligman, Martin E. P. *Authentic Happiness: Using the New Positive Psychology to Realize Your Potential for Lasting Fulfillment*. New York: Atria Books, 2004.

21 GENEALOGY

Drake, Pamela J. "Findings from the Fullerton Genealogy Study." Master's thesis, California State University, 2001.

Fischer, Peter, et al. "The Ancestor Effect: Thinking about Our Genetic Origin Enhances Intellectual Performance." *European Journal of Social Psychology* 41, no. 1 (2011): 11–16.

Fivush, Robyn, M. Duke, and J. G. Bohanek. "Do You Know...: The Power of Family History in Adolescent Identity and Well-Being." *Journal of Family Life* (2010): 748–769.

"The Poetry of Laurence Overmire." Home.comcast.net. Accessed July 21, 2015. http://home.comcast.net/~overmirepoetry/site/.

22 GRATITUDE

Ginzberg, Louis. *Legends of the Bible*. Philadelphia: Jewish Publication Society of America, 1975.

Hoffman, Edward. *The Right to Be Human: A Biography of Abraham Maslow*, 2nd ed. New York: McGraw-Hill, 1999.

Seligman, Martin E. P., et al. "Positive Psychology Progress: Empirical Validation of Interventions." *American Psychologist* 60, no. 5 (2005): 410–421.

Tsang, Jo-Ann. "Gratitude and Prosocial Behaviour: An Experimental Test of Gratitude." *Cognition & Emotion* 20, no. 1 (2006): 138–148.

23 HUMOR AND LAUGHTER

Freud, Sigmund. *Wit and Its Relation to the Unconscious*. Translated by A. A. Brill. Mineola, N.Y.: Dover, 2011.

Hoffman, Edward. *The Drive for Self: Alfred Adler and the Founding of Individual Psychology*. Reading, Mass.: Addison-Wesley, 1994.

Martin, Rod A., et al. "Individual Differences in Uses of Humor and Their Relation to Psychological Well-Being: Development of the Humor Styles Questionnaire." *Journal of Research in Personality* 37, no. 1 (2003): 48–75.

24 KINDNESS

Dalai Lama. *A Policy of Kindness: An Anthology of Writings by and About the Dalai Lama*, edited by Disney Piburn. Ithaca, N.Y.: Snow Lion, 1990.

Dalai Lama, with Howard Cutler. *The Art of Happiness: A Handbook for Living*. New York: Riverhead, 1998.

Layous, Kristin, et al. "Kindness Counts: Prompting Prosocial Behavior in Preadolescents Boosts Peer Acceptance and Well-Being." *PLOS ONE* 7, no. 12 (2012). http://journals.plos.org/plosone/article?id=10.1371/journal.pone.0051380.

Lyubomirsky, Sonja, and Lee Ross. "Hedonic Consequences of Social Comparison: A Contrast of Happy and Unhappy People." *Journal of Personality and Social Psychology* 73 (1997): 1141–1157.

Nolen-Hoeksema, Susan, Blair E. Wisco, and Sonja Lyubomirsky. "Rethinking Rumination." *Perspectives on Psychological Science* 3, no. 5 (2008): 400–424.

Otake, Keiko, et al. "Happy People Become Happier through Kindness: A Counting Kindness Intervention." *Journal of Happiness Studies* 7 (2006): 361–375.

Tsvetkova, Milena, and Michael W. Macy. "The Social Contagion of Generosity." *PLOS ONE* 9, no. 2 (2014): e87275.

25 KNITTING

Geda, Yonas E., et al. "Engaging in Cognitive Activities, Aging, and Mild Cognitive Impairment: A Population-Based Study." *Journal of Neuropsychiatry and Clinical Neurosciences* 23, no. 2 (2011): 149–154.

Kaneshiro, Susan. Personal communication to author. May 14, 2015.

"Knitting Interview: Betsan Corkhill of Stitchlinks." *Woman's Weekly*. Accessed July 21, 2015. http://www.womansweekly.com/knitting-crochet/knitting-interview-betsan-corkhill-of-stitchlinks.

Riley, Jill, Betsan Corkhill, and Clare Morris. "The Benefits of Knitting for Personal and Social Well-Being in Adulthood: Findings from an International Survey." *British Journal of Occupational Therapy* 76, no. 2 (2013): 50–57.

26 LEARNING A FOREIGN LANGUAGE

Jaggi, Maya. "George and His Dragons." *Guardian*. Last modified March 17, 2001.

Keysar, Boaz, Sayuri L. Hayakawa, and Sun Gyu An. "The Foreign-Language Effect: Thinking in a Foreign Tongue Reduces Decision Biases." *Psychological Science* 23, no. 6 (2012): 661–668.

Mohn, Tanya. "Learning a New Language on Location." *New York Times*, May 9, 2012. Accessed July 27, 2015. http://www.nytimes.com/2012/05/10/business/retirementspecial/learning-a-new-language-on-location.html?_r=0.

27 LIFE METAPHORS

Hoffman, Edward. *"Le Metafore della Vita." Psicologia Contemporanea*, January 8, 2014, 6–11.

Hoffman, Edward, and Catalina Acosta-Orozco. "Life-Metaphors among Colombian Leadership Students: Core Values and Educational Implications." *College Student Journal* 49, no. 3 (2015): 438–446.

Hoffman, Edward, Catalina Acosto-Orozco, and William Compton. "Life-Metaphors among Colombian Medical Students: Uncovering Core Values and Educational Implications." *College Student Journal* 49, no. 3 (2015): 590–598.

Lakoff, George. *Metaphors We Live By*, 2nd ed. Chicago: University of Chicago Press, 2003.

28 MENTORING

Erikson, Erik H. *Childhood and Society.* New York: W. W. Norton, 1950.

Erikson, Erik H., Joan M. Erikson, and Helen Q. Kivnick. *Vital Involvement in Old Age.* New York: W. W. Norton, 1986.

Goldin, Paul Rakita. *Rituals of the Way: The Philosophy of Xunzi.* Chicago: Open Court Press, 1999.

Jones, B. K., and D. P. McAdams. "Becoming Generative: Socializing Influences Recalled in Life Stories in Late Midlife." *Journal of Adult Development* 20, no. 3 (2013): 158–172.

Kotre, John. *Outliving the Self: Generativity and the Interpretation of Lives.* Baltimore: Johns Hopkins University Press, 1984.

McAdams, Dan P., and Ed de St. Aubin, eds. *Generativity and Adult Development: How and Why We Care for the Next Generation.* Washington, D.C.: American Psychological Association, 1998.

29 MINDFULNESS

Benson, Herbert. *The Relaxation Response.* New York: Morrow, 1975.

Burpee, Leslie C., and Ellen J. Langer. "Mindfulness and Marital Satisfaction." *Journal of Adult Development* 12, no. 1 (2005): 43–51.

Doyle, Sir Arthur Conan. *The Hound of the Baskervilles.* North Charleston, S.C.: CreateSpace Independent Publishing Platform, 2014.

Feinberg, Cara. "The Mindfulness Chronicles: On 'The Psychology of Possibility.'" *Harvard Magazine,* September 2010. Accessed July 27, 2015. http://harvardmagazine.com/2010/09/the-mindfulness-chronicles.

Kabat-Zinn, Jon, Leslie Lipworth, and Robert Burney. "The Clinical Use of Mindfulness Meditation for the Self-Regulation of Chronic Pain." *Journal of Behavioral Medicine* 8 (1985): 163–190.

Langer, Ellen. *Mindfulness.* Reading, Mass.: Perseus, 1989.

Perls, Fritz, Ralph F. Hefferline, and Paul Goodman. *Gestalt Therapy: Excitement and Growth in the Human Personality.* New York: Dell, 1951.

Varela, Keosha. "Are You Living Mindfully or Mindlessly?" *The Aspen Institute,* July 30, 2014. Accessed July 27, 2015. http://www.aspeninstitute.org/about/blog/are-you-living-mindfully-or-mindlessly.

30 MORAL ELATION

Algoe, Sara B., and Jonathan Haidt. "Witnessing Excellence in Action: The 'Other-Praising' Emotions of Elevation, Gratitude, and Admiration." *Journal of Positive Psychology* 4, no. 2 (2009): 105–127.

Farsides, Tom, Danelle Pettman, and Louise Tourle. "Inspiring Altruism: Reflecting on the Personal Relevance of Emotionally Evocative Prosocial Media Characters." *Journal of Applied Social Psychology* 43, no. 1 (2013): 2251–2258.

Haidt, Jonathan. "The Positive Emotion of Elevation." *Journal of Organizational Behavior* 3, no. 3 (2000b).

Niemiec, Ryan M. *Positive Psychology at the Movies: Using Films to Build Character Strengths and Well-Being*. Boston: Hogrefe Publishing, 2013.

Schnall, Simone, Jean Roper, and Daniel M. T. Fessler. "Elevation Leads to Altruistic Behavior." *Psychological Science* 21, no. 3 (2010): 315–320.

31 NOSTALGIA

Hirsch, Alan. "Nostalgia: A Neuropsychiatric Understanding." In *Advances in Consumer Research* 19, edited by John F. Sherry Jr. and Brian Sternthal. Provo, Utah.: Association of Consumer Research, 1992, 390–395.

Wildschut, Tim, Constantine Sedikides, Jamie Arndt, and Clay Routledge. "Nostalgia: Content, Triggers, Functions." *Journal of Personality and Social Psychology* 91, no. 5 (2006): 975.

Zhou, Xinyue, Constantine Sedikides, Tim Wildschut, and Ding-Guo Gao. "Counteracting Loneliness: On the Restorative Function of Nostalgia." *Psychological Science* 19, no. 10 (2008), 1023–1029.

32 OVERCOMING REGRETS

Adams, Guy. "Steve Jobs' Final Wish: To Get to Know His Children before It Was Too Late." *The Independent*, October 8, 2015. Accessed July 27, 2015. http://www.independent.co.uk/news/world/americas/steve-jobs-final-wish-to-get-to-know-his-children-before-it-was-too-late-2367355.html.

Bauer, Isabelle, and Carsten Wrosch. "Making Up for Lost Opportunities: The Protective Role of Downward Social Comparisons for Coping with Regrets across Adulthood." *Personality and Social Psychology Bulletin* 37, no. 2 (2011): 215–228.

Mansfield, Katherine. *The Collected Stories of Katherine Mansfield*. Ware, UK: Wordsworth Editions, 2006.

Wrosch, Carsten, Isabelle Bauer, Gregory E. Miller, and Sonia Lupien. "Regret Intensity, Diurnal Cortisol Secretion, and Physical Health in Older Individuals: Evidence for Directional Effects and Protective Factors." *Psychology and Aging* 22, no. 2 (2007): 319.

Zhou, Xinyue, Constantine Sedikides, Tim Wildschut, and Ding-Guo Gao. "Counteracting Loneliness on the Restorative Function of Nostalgia." *Psychological Science* 19, no. 10 (2008): 1023–1029.

33 PEAK EXPERIENCES

Hoffman, Edward. *The Right to Be Human: A Biography of Abraham Maslow.* New York: McGraw-Hill, 1999.

———. "Peak-Experiences in Japanese Youth." *Japanese Journal of Humanistic Psychology* 21, no. 1 (2003): 112–121.

Hoffman, Edward, et al. "Retrospective Peak-Experiences among Chinese Young Adults in Hong Kong." *Journal of Humanistic Counseling* 53, no. 1 (2014): 34–46.

Hoffman, Edward, and Fernando Oritz, "Youthful Peak Experiences in Cross-Cultural Perspective: Implications for Educators and Counselors." In *The International Handbook for Education for Spirituality, Care & Well-Being*, edited by L. Francis, D. Scott, M. de Souza, and J. Norman, 469-489. New York: Springer, 2009.

Maslow, Abraham H. "Cognition of Being in the Peak Experiences." *Journal of Humanistic Psychology* 1, no. 2 (1959): 1–11.

34 PETS

"About Pet Partners." *Pet Partners.* Accessed July 2015. https://petpartners .org/about-us/

Butler, Robert A. "The Effect of Deprivation of Visual Incentives on Visual Exploration Motivation in Monkeys." *Journal of Comparative and Psychological Psychology* 50, no. 2 (1957): 177–179.

Hoffman, Jan. "The Science of Puppy-Dog Eyes." *New York Times*, April 16, 2015. Accessed July 27, 2015. http://nyti.ms/1FZVrwL.

Homer. *The Odyssey.* Translated by Robert Fagles. New York: Penguin, 2006.

"ISAAT History." *International Society for Animal-Assisted Therapy.* Accessed July 2015. http://aat-isaat.org/index.php?option= com_content&view=article&id=4&Itemid=5.

McConnell, Allen R., et al. "Friends with Benefits: On the Positive Consequences of Pet Ownership." *Journal of Personality and Social Psychology* 101, no. 6 (2011): 1239.

Morrison, Michelle L. "Health Benefits of Animal-Assisted Interventions." *Complementary Health Practice Review* 12, no. 1 (2007): 51–62.

35 PHOTOGRAPHY

Kellock, Anne. "Through the Lens: Accessing Children's Voices in New Zealand on Well-Being." *International Journal of Inclusive Education* 15, no. 1 (2011): 41–55.

Kurtz, Jaime L., and Sonja Lyubomirsky. "Happiness Promotion: Using Mindful Photography to Increase Positive Emotion and Appreciation." In *Activities for Teaching Positive Psychology: A Guide for Instructors*, edited by Jeffrey J. Froh and Acacia C. Parks, 133–136. Washington, D.C.: American Psychological Association, 2013.

"Minor White." *Lee Gallery.* Accessed July 27, 2015. http://www.leegallery.com/minor-white/minor-white-biography.

"Minor White American Photographer." *Anne Darling Photography.* Accessed July 27, 2015. http://www.annedarlingphotography.com/minor-white.html.

Nic Gabhainn, Saoirse, and Jane Sixsmith. "Children Photographing Well-Being: Facilitating Participation in Research." *Children & Society* 20, no. 4 (2006): 249–259.

"Thank You." *International Conference on Photography and Therapeutic Photography.* Accessed July 27, 2015. http://congress.utu.fi/phototherapy08/.

Weiser, Judy. *Phototherapy Techniques: Exploring the Secrets of Personal Snapshots and Family Albums*, 2nd ed. Vancouver, B.C.: PhotoTherapy Centre Press, 1999.

White, Minor. "The Camera Mind and Eye." In *Photographers on Photography*, edited by Nathan Lyons. Englewood Cliffs, N.J.: Prentice Hall, 1966.

36 POETRY

Boone, Beth C., and Linda G. Castillo. "The Use of Poetry Therapy with Domestic Violence Counselors Experiencing Secondary Posttraumatic Stress Disorder Symptoms." *Journal of Poetry Therapy* 21, no. 1 (2008): 3–14.

Brillantes-Evangelista, Grace. "An Evaluation of Visual Arts and Poetry as Therapeutic Interventions with Abused Adolescents." *Arts in Psychotherapy* 40, no. 1 (2013): 71–84.

Croom, Adam M. "The Practice of Poetry and the Psychology of Well-Being." *Journal of Poetry Therapy* 28, no. 1 (2015): 21–41.

Heimes, Silke. "State of Poetry Therapy Research (Review)." *Arts in Psychotherapy* 38, no. 1 (2011): 1–8.

Shelley, Percy Bysshe. "A Defence of Poetry." In *English Essays: Sidney to Macaulay. The Harvard Classics*. 1909–14, edited by Charles Eliot. Indianapolis: Collier, 1909.

Trethewey, Natasha. "Necessary Utterance: On Poetry as a Cultural Force." *Virginia Quarterly Review* 90, no. 1 (2014): 54–61.

37 POWER NAPPING

Alleyne, Richard. "AAAS: A Nap After Lunch Boosts the Brain's Learning Capacity." *Telegraph*, February 21, 2010. Accessed July 27, 2015. http://www.telegraph.co.uk/news/health/news/7285527/AAAS-A-nap-after-lunch-boosts-the-brains-learning-capacity.html.

Anwar, Yasmin. "An Afternoon Nap Markedly Boosts the Brain's Learning Capacity." *Berkeley News*, February 22, 2010. Accessed August 22, 2015. http://news.berkeley.edu/2010/02/22/naps_boost_learning_capacity.

Delo, Cotton. "Why Companies Are Cozying Up to Napping at Work." *Fortune*, August 18, 2011. Accessed July 27, 2015. http://fortune.com/2011/08/18/why-companies-are-cozying-up-to-napping-at-work.

Desai, Alap Naik. "Albert Einstein, among Other Great Minds, Proved the Efficacy of Micro-Naps." *Inquisitor*. Accessed July 27, 2015. http://www.inquisitr.com/1754670/albert-einstein-among-other-great-minds-proved-the-efficacy-of-micro-naps.

Gómez, Rebecca L., Richard R. Bootzin, and Lynn Nadel. "Naps Promote Abstraction in Language-Learning Infants." *Psychological Science* 17, no. 8 (2006): 670–674.

McKay, Brett, and Kate McKay. "The Napping Habits of 8 Famous Men." *The Art of Manliness*, March 14, 2011. Accessed July 27, 2015. http://www.artofmanliness.com/2011/03/14/the-napping-habits-of-8-famous-men.

Tietzel, Amber J. "The Recuperative Value of Brief and Ultra-Brief Naps on Alertness and Cognitive Performance." *Journal of Sleep Research* 11, no. 3 (2002): 213–18.

38 PRAYER

James, William. *The Varieties of Religious Experience*. New York: Penguin, 1982.

Lambert, Nathaniel M., et al. "Motivating Change in Relationships: Can Prayer Increase Forgiveness?" *Psychological Science* 21, no. 1 (2010): 126.

Singer, Isaac Bashevis, and Richard Burgin. *Conversations with Isaac Bashevis Singer*. New York: Farrar, Straus & Giroux, 1978.

Whittington, Brandon L., and Steven J. Scher. "Prayer and Subjective Well-Being: An Examination of Six Different Types of Prayer." *International Journal for the Psychology of Religion* 20, no. 1 (2010): 59–68.

39 RESTORATIVE NATURE

Berman, Marc G., John Jonides, and Stephen Kaplan. "The Cognitive Benefits of Interacting with Nature." *Psychological Science* 19, no. 12 (2008): 1207–1212.

Berto, Rita. "The Role of Nature in Coping with Psycho-Physiological Stress: A Literature Review on Restorativeness." *Behavioral Sciences* 4, no. 4 (2014): 394–409.

Hartig, David. Personal communication to author. March 15, 2015.

Hartig, Terry, Richard Mitchell, Sjerp De Vries, and Howard Frumkin. "Nature and Health." *Annual Review of Public Health* 35 (2014): 207–228.

Keniger, Lucy E., Kevin J. Gaston, Katherine N. Irvine, and Richard A. Fuller. "What Are the Benefits of Interacting with Nature?" *International Journal of Environmental Research and Public Health* 10, no. 3 (2013): 913–935.

Muir, John. *The Yosemite*. North Charleston, S.C.: CreateSpace Independent Publishing Platform, 2014.

40 SAVORING

Harrar, Sari. "How to Double Your Happiness." *Prevention*, May 3, 2013. Accessed July 27, 2015. http://www.prevention.com/mind-body/emotional-health/double-your-happiness-through-savoring.

Hurley, Daniel B., and Paul Kwon. "Results of a Study to Increase Savoring the Moment: Differential Impact on Positive and Negative Outcomes." *Journal of Happiness Studies* 13, no. 4 (2012): 579–588.

Jose, Paul E., Bee T. Lim, and Fred B. Bryant. "Does Savoring Increase Happiness? A Daily Diary Study." *Journal of Positive Psychology* 7, no. 3 (2012): 176–187.

41 SELF-COMPASSION

Phillips, Wendy J., and Susan J. Ferguson. "Self-Compassion: A Resource for Positive Aging." *Journals of Gerontology Series B: Psychological Sciences and Social Sciences* 68, no. 4 (2013): 529–539.

Van Nuys, David. "An Interview with Kristin Neff, PhD, on Self-Compassion." The website of Emergence Health Network. Accessed July 27, 2015. http://www.info.emergencehealthnetwork.org/poc/view_doc.php?type=doc&id=43061.

42 SELF-DISCLOSURE

Antill, John K., and Sandra Cotton. "Self Disclosure between Husbands and Wives: Its Relationship to Sex Roles and Marital Happiness." *Australian Journal of Psychology* 39, no. 1 (1987): 11–24.

Austen, Jane. *Pride and Prejudice.* North Charleston, S.C.: CreateSpace Independent Publishing Platform, 2014.

Horenstein, Veronica Diaz-Peralta, and Jerrold L. Downey. "A Cross-Cultural Investigation of Self-Disclosure." *North American Journal of Psychology* 5, no. 3 (2003): 373–386.

Jourard, Sidney. "Healthy Personality and Self-Disclosure." *Mental Hygiene* 43 no. 4 (1959): 499–507.

Schwartz, Audrey L., Renée V. Galliher, and Melanie M. Domenech Rodríguez. "Self-Disclosure in Latinos' Intercultural and Intracultural Friendships and Acquaintanceships: Links with Collectivism, Ethnic Identity, and Acculturation." *Cultural Diversity and Ethnic Minority Psychology* 17, no. 1 (2011): 116.

Trepte, Sabine, and Leonard Reinecke. "The Reciprocal Effects of Social Network Site Use and the Disposition for Self-Disclosure: A Longitudinal Study." *Computers in Human Behavior* 29, no. 3 (2013): 1102–1112.

43 SENSE OF WONDER

Einstein, Albert. "Letter of 1950." *New York Times*, March 29, 1972.

———. *Einstein on Cosmic Religion and Other Opinions and Aphorisms.* Mineola N.Y.: Dover Publications, 2009.

Hartwell, David G. *Age of Wonders: Exploring the World of Science Fiction.* New York: Tor Books, 1996.

Maslow, Abraham. *Farther Reaches of Human Nature.* New York: Viking, 1971.

Stolberg, Tonie L. "W(h)ither the Sense of Wonder of Pre-Service Primary Teachers when Teaching Science? A Preliminary Study of Their Personal Experiences." *Teaching and Teacher Education* 24, no. 8 (2008): 1958–1964.

Wordsworth, William. *The Collected Poems of William Wordsworth (Wordsworth Poetry Library).* Ware, UK: Wordsworth Editions Ltd., 1998.

44 TAI CHI

Callahan, Leigh, et al. "Evaluation of Tai Chi Effectiveness for People with Arthritis." *Arthritis & Rheumatism* 62, (2010).

"Tai Chi: An Introduction." *National Center for Complementary and Integrative Health.com*, August 2010. Last accessed July 27, 2015. https://nccih.nih.gov/health/taichi/introduction.htm.

Wang, Chenchen, et al. "Tai Chi on Psychological Well-Being: Systematic Review and Meta-Analysis." *BMC Complementary and Alternative Medicine* 10, no. 1 (2010): 23.

Wise, R. A. *Wise Quotes of Wisdom: A Lifetime Collection of Quotes, Sayings, Philosophies, Viewpoints, and Thoughts*. Bloomington, Ind.: AuthorHouse, 2011.

45 TEARS OF JOY

Hoffman, Edward, and Alison Tran. "Tears of Joy: The Impact on Resilience and Health." Paper presentation, Society for Behavioral Medicine, 35th Annual Meeting & Scientific Sessions. Philadelphia, 2014.

Hoffman, Edward, Alison Tran, and Jenniffer González-Mujica. "Tears of Joy: A Cross-Cultural Comparison." Unpublished manuscript, 2015.

Hoffman, Edward, Neeta Relwani Garg, and Jenniffer González-Mujica. "Tears of Joy in India." *Indian Journal of Positive Psychology* 4, no. 2 (2013): 212–217.

Poe, Edgar Allan. "The Poetic Principle." In *The Harvard Classics. 1909–14*, edited by Charles Eliot. Indianapolis: Collier, 1909.

46 TIME AFFLUENCE

Elkind, David. *The Hurried Child: Growing Up Too Fast Too Soon*. Reading, Mass.: Addison-Wesley, 1990.

Kasser, Tim. Personal communication to author. March 16, 2015.

Kasser, Tim, and Kennon M. Sheldon. "Time Affluence as a Path toward Personal Happiness and Ethical Business Practice: Empirical Evidence from Four Studies." *Journal of Business Ethics* 84, no. 2 (2009): 243–255.

Mogilner, Cassie. "You'll Feel Less Rushed if You Give Time Away." *Harvard Business Review* 90, no. 9 (2012): 28–29.

Mogilner, Cassie, Zoë Chance, and Michael I. Norton. "Giving Time Gives You Time." *Psychological Science* 23, no. 10 (2012): 1233–1238.

Perlow, Leslie A. "The Time Famine: Toward a Sociology of Work Time," *Administrative Science Quarterly* 44, no. 1 (1999): 57–81.

Schor, Juliet. *The Overworked American: The Unexpected Decline of Leisure*. New York: Basic Books, 1993.

Tolkien, J. R. R. *The Fellowship of the Ring: Being the First Part of the Lord of the Rings*. New York: Houghton Mifflin Harcourt, 2012.

REFERENCES

∾

47 TRAVEL

Filep, Sebastian. "Flow, Sightseeing, Satisfaction, and Personal Development: Exploring Relationships via Positive Psychology." In: *Proceedings of the 17th Annual CAUTHE Conference* (2007).

Filep, Sebastian, and Philip Pearce. "A Blueprint for Tourist Experience and Fulfillment Research." *Tourist Experience and Fulfillment: Insights from Positive Psychology* 31 (2013): 223–232.

Jia, Lile, Edward R. Hirt, and Samuel C. Karpen. "Lessons from a Faraway Land: The Effect of Spatial Distance on Creative Cognition." *Journal of Experimental Social Psychology* 45, no. 5 (2009): 1127–1131.

Maddux, William W., and Adam D. Galinsky. "Cultural Borders and Mental Barriers: The Relationship between Living Abroad and Creativity." *Journal of Personality and Social Psychology* 96, no. 5 (2009): 1047.

Tadmor, Carmit T., Adam D. Galinsky, and William W. Maddux. "Getting the Most Out of Living Abroad: Biculturalism and Integrative Complexity as Key Drivers of Creative and Professional Success." *Journal of Personality and Social Psychology* 103, no. 3 (2012): 520.

Twain, Mark. *The Innocents Abroad*. London: Wordsworth Editions, 2010.

48 VOLUNTEERING

Atkins, Robert, Daniel Hart, and Thomas M. Donnelly. "The Association of Childhood Personality Type with Volunteering During Adolescence." *Merrill-Palmer Quarterly* 51, no. 2 (April 2005): 145–162.

Binder, Martin, and Andreas Freytag. "Volunteering, Subjective Well-Being, and Public Policy." *Journal of Economic Psychology* 34 (2013): 97–119.

Kennedy, John F. Inaugural Address, United States Capitol, Washington, D.C., January 20, 1961.

Kuperminc, Gabriel P., Phyllis T. Holditch, and Joseph P. Allen. "Volunteering and Community Service in Adolescence." *Adolescent Medicine* 12, no. 3 (October 2001): 445–457.

Morrow-Howell, Nancy, et al. "Effects of Volunteering on the Well-Being of Older Adults." *The Journals of Gerontology Series B: Psychological Sciences and Social Sciences* 58, no. 3 (2003): S137–S145.

Schreier, Hannah M. C., Kimberly A. Schonert-Reichl, and Edith Chen. "Effect of Volunteering on Risk Factors for Cardiovascular Disease in Adolescents: A Randomized Controlled Trial." *JAMA Pediatrics* 167, no. 4 (2013): 327–332.

Thoits, Peggy A., and Lyndi N. Hewitt. "Volunteer Work and Well-Being." *Journal of Health and Social Behavior* 42 (June 2001): 115–131.

49 WISDOM

Ardelt, Monika. "Wisdom and Life Satisfaction in Old Age." *Journals of Gerontology Series B: Psychological Sciences and Social Sciences* 52, no. 1 (1997): 15–27.

Baltes, Paul B., and Ursula M. Staudinger. "Wisdom: A Metaheuristic (Pragmatic) to Orchestrate Mind and Virtue toward Excellence." *American Psychologist* 55, no. 1 (2000): 122.

Duane, Daniel. "The Socratic Shrink." *New York Times*, March 21, 2004. Accessed July 27, 2015. http://www.nytimes.com/2004/03/21/magazine/the-socratic-shrink.html.

Grossmann, Igor, et al. "A Route to Well-Being: Intelligence versus Wise Reasoning." *Journal of Experimental Psychology: General 142*, no. 3 (2013): 944–953.

Wright, Robert. "Does Wisdom Bring Happiness (or Vice Versa)?" *Atlantic*, August 9, 2012. Accessed July 27, 2015. http://www.theatlantic.com/health/archive/2012/08/does-wisdom-bring-happiness-or-vice-versa/260949/.

50 ZEN MEDITATION

Austin, James H. *Zen and the Brain: Toward an Understanding of Meditation and Consciousness.* Cambridge, Mass.: MIT Press, 1998.

———. *Zen-Brain Reflections.* Cambridge, Mass.: MIT Press, 2006.

———. *Selfless Insight: Zen and the Meditative Transformation of Consciousness.* Cambridge, Mass.: MIT Press, 2009.

Schnall, Marianne. "Exclusive Interview with Zen Master Thich Nhat Hanh." *Huffington Post*, May 21, 2010. Accessed July 27, 2015. http://www.huffingtonpost.com/marianne-schnall/beliefs-buddhism-exclusiv_b_577541.html.